Are you sitting uncomfortably? Windy Dryden, Live and Uncut

Windy Dryden

PCCS BOOKS
Ross-on-Wye

First published in 1998

PCCS BOOKS
Llangarron
Ross-on-Wye
HR9 6PT
Tel. (01989) 77 07 07
Fax. (01989) 77 07 00
e-mail books@pccs.telme.com

Are you sitting uncomfortably?
Windy Dryden, Live and Uncut

ISBN 1 898059 18 7

Cover design by Denis Postle
Printed by Redwood Books, Trowbridge, Wiltshire.

contents

introduction   i

1   thirty ways to improve counselling   1

2   keeping the door open: the need for counselling in a complex, ever changing world   25

3   why I no longer practise person-centred therapy and psychodynamic therapy: some personal reflections   35

4   rational emotive behaviour therapy: why I practise an approach to counselling that is unpopular   45

5   the counsellor as educator: promise, possibilities and problems   59

6   feel better, get worse; feel worse, get better   75

7   rationality and Relate   87

8   why I do not help my clients to raise their self-esteem   99

9   influence your clients for their health's sake: a rational emotive perspective   111

10   why self-help books don't work   125

11   rationality, outrageous ideas and sensitivity   137

12   looking for the good in Hitler and acknowledging the bad in Mother Teresa   151

index   167

I dedicate this book to the memory of Albert Kushlik who died last year. I met Albert when he attended one of my REBT training programmes in the early 1980s and we remained friendly ever since. Albert was perhaps best known for his pioneering work with people with severe learning difficulties and challenging behaviour. I will particularly remember him for his compassion which touched many who knew him both personally and professionally.

introduction

As many writers have noted before me, one of the best ways of discovering what you think about a topic is to write about it. I have also found that one of the best ways of knowing what I think about a subject is to speak on it. This book presents twelve invited talks I have given in recent years on a number of themes. In general, these talks were given in response to invitations to address a variety of audiences. Most of these audiences were professional, but several of the lectures were broadly advertised and open to members of the public as well as to counselling professionals and students of counselling.

In the past, whenever I was invited to give a lecture I regarded it as something of a chore and talked off the cuff without much preparation. Then I realised that I was short-changing both myself and, in particular, my audience. So in recent years I subjected myself to the discipline of preparing and reading a formally presented paper whether I was giving a keynote address at an international conference (Chapter 11) or a talk to a local audience at a bookshop (Chapter 10). The discipline of preparing a timed lecture has both sharpened and clarified my thinking in a number of key areas of counselling and psychotherapy. I hope you, the reader, benefit as much from reading these lectures as I gained from preparing and delivering them.

Windy Dryden
London and East Sussex

1

thirty ways to improve counselling

This paper was delivered as the tenth Hartop Lecture and took place at Grey College, University of Durham, on 5 May 1993. The Hartop Lectures are given annually in memory of Ben Hartop, Senior Lecturer in Education at Durham, who helped to pioneer Guidance and Counselling in Initial Teacher Training. It was planned to terminate the Hartop Lectures after ten years, but the organising committee, encouraged by the packed audience at my lecture, decided to continue to arrange them.

The subject of the lecture was based on a book I wrote with Colin Feltham entitled *Developing the Practice of Counselling* (Sage, 1994) and I wish to acknowledge Colin's influence on the lecture. I also wish to thank the organising committee for giving permission to include the paper in this collection.

There are many different approaches to counselling, and consequently it is difficult to gain a consensual view concerning how counsellors can improve their practice. None the less, in this lecture I intend to outline thirty ways in which counsellors from most orientations can improve the effectiveness of their work. I have divided these thirty points into five sections.

I
Improvements in Forming an Ethical Alliance with Clients

1. Develop the use of contracts

One of the easiest ways for counsellors to improve their work is by developing the use of contracts with their clients. By this I do not mean that legally binding contracts should be established where one or other of the people concerned can be sued if the contract is broken. Rather, I am suggesting that counsellors develop a shared understanding with their clients and come to an explicit agreement concerning the nature of the work that they are going to undertake together.

To this end, some counsellors have prepared written handouts which they give to prospective clients. These handouts contain information about the counsellor, her training, a statement about her approach to the work of counselling, the ethical code to which she adheres and other pertinent information. Such information helps prospective clients to make informed judgements about whether or not they wish to consult this particular counsellor.

In the field of counselling a distinction can be made between a business contract and a therapeutic contract. A business contract contains agreements that the counsellor makes with her client about issues such as the frequency of consultations, where the consultations will occur, the fee to be paid and the terms of the counsellor's cancellation policy.

A therapeutic contract, on the other hand, includes such points as the goals that the counsellor and client are working towards, a shared conceptualisation of the client's concerns and which therapeutic tasks or techniques the counsellor and client are going to use in the service of the client's goals. It is important to realise that the therapeutic contract does not include promises to achieve specific outcomes.

Most contracts that counsellors seek to negotiate with their clients include the issue of confidentiality and its limits. In my view, this issue straddles the business and therapeutic contract in that it does not easily fit into either single category. In this respect, some interesting American research has shown that clients desire more information about confidentiality and its limits than counsellors tend to provide (Miller & Thelen, 1986). Indeed, this research showed that clients expect more exceptions to complete confidentiality than they encounter. The BAC

Code of Ethics and Practice stresses that accepted limits to confidentiality occur when clients are either at risk to themselves or constitute a risk to the welfare of other people. My own experience is that, when this is explained to clients clearly and professionally, they understand the reasons for these limits and are happy to agree to them.

It is important to stress that the contracts that I have described are subject to negotiation between counsellor and client. As such, therefore they can be renegotiated during the counselling process. They are not set in stone. The explicit nature of the discussions that occur during the development of these contracts helps move counselling away from being a mysterious process towards being a comprehensible, collaborative process which empowers the client.

2. Develop and maintain the reflection process

The reflection process in counselling occurs when counsellor and client step back from the work that they are undertaking together and reflect on and discuss this work. It is, if you like, a process of talking about the process of counselling. I wish to stress that I am not suggesting that counsellors do this in an overly anxious way, but that they take sincere steps to involve their clients in a process of mutual feedback.

Various psychoanalytic theorists have distinguished between the observing ego and the experiencing ego. Such a distinction is particularly relevant here. In the reflection process, the observing ego of the client and the observing ego of the counsellor step back and talk about what the experiencing egos of both of them have encountered. In some approaches to counselling, namely cognitive therapy, this is done routinely at the end of every counselling session. Thus, a cognitive therapist will ask the client at the end of a session 'Can you tell me what about today's session was helpful to you and what was unhelpful for you?' While counsellor and client are more likely to refer to the reflection process at the end of a session and formally, in structured review sessions, they can refer to this process at any time during counselling.

I have learnt a great deal from inviting a client to reflect on the process of counselling, and as a result of feedback I have received from my clients I have made important modifications to my counselling approach. I doubt whether I would have made such changes if I had not initiated and nurtured the reflection process. Herbert Strean (1959), a psychoanalytic author, has originated a term that is particularly relevant to what I am talking about. He calls the client 'a consultant' – a term I particularly like in that it empowers the client and stresses that he or she can actively and productively contribute to the counselling process.

Counsellors can use the reflection process to clarify a number of issues. They can use it, for example, to determine whether or not the client is in the most useful therapeutic arena. It may transpire, when discussing the client's experience of counselling, that seeing the client in individual counselling may not be as helpful to the client as seeing him with his spouse in couple counselling. Knowing this can lead to useful and substantive alterations in counselling strategy.

Another issue that can be referred to the reflection process concerns changes in the therapeutic goals that clients have negotiated with their counsellors. Without a forum where the changing nature of these goals can be discussed, it may well be that counsellors assume that the goals that they negotiate with their clients at the outset of counselling are still relevant in the middle phase of counselling. Other issues that can be discussed in the reflection process concern whether or not the counsellor is the best person to help the client, the accuracy of the counsellor's conceptualisation of the client's problems, and the pacing of the work that is being done (a subject of which I have more to say later).

3. Identify and use the most helpful arena for clients

I alluded to this issue briefly in the previous section and will not elaborate on it here. It is important to stress that not every client who seeks counselling will be most helped by working in the arena of individual counselling. What I am suggesting is that counsellors need to be aware of the advantages and disadvantages of different therapeutic arenas so that a productive match between client and therapeutic arena can be made.

Let me give some examples of how different clients may be suited to different arenas. In my experience, individual counselling is the most suitable arena for clients who are particularly concerned about confidentiality and for vulnerable clients who need to develop a one-to-one trusting relationship with the counsellor. In addition, individual counselling is the arena of choice when clients need an ongoing and extended in-depth exploration of intrapsychic issues.

However, if a client has a relationship problem with a named individual such as a spouse, then the counsellor should carefully consider using the arena of couple counselling, particularly if the client's partner is willing to be involved in counselling. Family counselling is particularly indicated when more than one significant other is involved in the 'identified' client's problem, whereas group counselling is frequently the arena of choice for clients who have difficulties forming and developing interpersonal relationships in general, who experience themselves as alienated or who consider that they are the only individual in the world with a particular type of problem.

Most counselling takes place in the arena of individual counselling. However tempting it may be, therefore, to suggest to all clients that they be seen in this arena, to do so will limit the usefulness of counselling for a significant number of clients.

4. Make suitable referrals in clients' best interests

It is tempting for counsellors to believe that they can help everyone who seeks their services. This is especially true for keen and enthusiastic trainees. However, experience teaches us that it is important to be humble in this field and to ask two questions of oneself: (i) 'Am I the best person to help this particular individual?' and (ii) 'Is there another counsellor who may be more helpful to this client?'

I have become sensitive to this issue because over the years I have received numerous telephone calls from potential female clients who think that I am a female counsellor and become quite confused when it becomes apparent that I am male. In such circumstances I refer these enquirers to a female counsellor.

There are a number of client concerns which, in my opinion, require a specialist referral. For example, it is really helpful for Holocaust survivors or their children to be seen by counsellors who have either survived the Holocaust themselves or have experienced growing up in a family where at least one member has been a Holocaust survivor. Indeed, clients who have the Holocaust in their background seem to want and in some cases expect to see a counsellor who has had some direct or indirect experience of this tragedy.

I am less impressed, however, by the argument that is strongly advanced in some areas of alcohol counselling that it is necessary to be a recovering alcoholic to work effectively with alcoholics. This seems to me too dogmatic, and, while I can appreciate that in certain circumstances with certain clients a counsellor who is himself a recovering alcoholic would be the helper of choice, to make a sweeping statement that all alcohol counsellors need to be recovering alcoholics seems to go too far.

While I am advocating making specialist referrals in certain circumstances, this does not obviate the need for counsellors to be knowledgeable in these areas, since they will be consulted by clients' who do not want such a specialist referral.

5. Form, maintain and vary different therapeutic bonds with different clients

While it is commonly agreed that the bond formed and developed between client and counsellor is a primary healing agent in the process of counselling, it is less well accepted that different clients may require different bonds with their counsellors. As such, it is important for counsellors to become flexible in the way they relate with their clients – to become what Arnold Lazarus (1981) has called 'an authentic chameleon', i.e. being able to 'change one's interpersonal style to meet the needs of clients but in a way that is congruent and authentic'. There are a number of important dimensions to consider here and I will mention just a few of them.

Some clients seem to value a self~disclosing counsellor who at poignant times in the counselling process shares her own experiences which are similar to those of her clients. While this can be a liberating and growth-promoting experience for such clients, other clients consider counsellor self-disclosure to be quite inappropriate. Earlier in my career I was working with an older woman and ventured to disclose a personal experience which I thought might be helpful to her. However, this was not the case and the client said to me: 'Young man, I am not paying this centre a lot of money to hear about your problems. Please focus on me.'

Some clients seem to do much better with an active–directive counsellor than with someone who is passive and less directive, and of course the reverse is also true. Some clients seem to respond well to judiciously timed, humorous interventions, while others do not.

Some clients are more influenced by the expertise of the counsellor, while others are more influenced by the counsellor's likeability. Some clients prefer to work with a counsellor who is warm and nurturing, while others prefer a more formal businesslike relationship, and, strange as it may seem, some clients respond very well to a sergeant major type of counsellor who is going to knock them into shape.

While I advocate interpersonal flexibility in forming and developing bonds with clients, it is important that counsellors do not strive to work beyond the limits of their flexibility. I do not want counsellors to put on an act.

6. Make use of formal review sessions

Earlier I discussed the importance of counsellors developing and maintaining the reflection process, by which I meant a process where counsellor and client stand back from the work and reflect on their experiences of this work. Holding formal, structured review sessions is a formal extension of the use of this process. The main purpose of holding such review sessions is for counsellor and client to gain a greater understanding of the progress that the client has made, either since counselling started or since the last formal structured review. In contemporary language, this is an important part of evaluation and audit.

Many counsellors do this particularly at the beginning of the counselling process, when they offer clients a period of time to experience counselling in order to judge whether or not it will be a valuable source of help. These counsellors may say: 'Let's meet for six sessions and then review where we have reached.' In doing so they are offering counselling on a trial basis. The important thing to convey to clients here is that it is a review of counselling that is to be conducted, rather than an assessment of the client. In this review, counsellor and client will focus on what the client has found helpful and unhelpful about the process so that they can develop a more productive relationship as a result. My own experience is that carrying out such periodic reviews gives both counsellor and client an opportunity to identify the client's reservations or doubts about the counselling process in a time-allocated manner. If this is sensitively handled, and if the counsellor can offer the client unconditional acceptance, the working alliance between them can be strengthened. If this is achieved, subsequent obstacles to client change can be identified and constructively dealt with.

II
Improvements in Understanding and Working with Effective Tasks and Goals

7. Monitor and improve the goal directedness of counselling

That perennial analysand, Woody Allen, was once asked how his analysis of twenty years was going; he replied, 'slowly' – and presumably aimlessly. There is a danger that counselling can become an end in itself where there is a timeless and directionless quality about the work. By contrast, effective counselling is more likely to occur when both counsellor and client have agreed explicitly or implicitly about the client's goals. I am not suggesting that counsellors become goal-directed with clients before the latter have had the opportunity to disclose their concerns. What I do want to stress is the important purposive aspects of counselling. I want counsellors to become sensitive and orientated towards client goals rather than to become obsessed with them.

Effective goals are those that are mutually agreed between counsellor and client and which stem logically from a shared understanding of the client's concerns and the issues that relate to these concerns. Goals are best phrased in a positive manner rather than indicating the absence of a negative state. For example, instead of a client's goal being 'not to feel anxious in social situations', the objective may be phrased thus: 'initially to feel concerned in social situations and later to feel relaxed in these situations'. In general, clients' goals need to be stated in their own language, to be as specific as possible and to be achievable. Thus, if a client states 'I want my husband to change', this is not a feasible goal since it is not within the client's control. In this situation, the counsellor might encourage the client to set as her goal changes in her own behaviour which may lead to changes in her husband's behaviour. It should be made clear, however, that the work the woman does with her counsellor may not directly lead to changes in her husband.

It goes without saying that productive goals need to be consistent with the client's value system and should not be based on the counsellor's value system. In addition, clients need to be helped to distinguish between goals that have been introjected, that is accepted uncritically from a significant other, and goals that have been explored, and owned. It is the latter to which the client is likely to show commitment. Counsellors need to recognise that client goals change over time, and it is important to monitor these goals and to identify what may lead to their shifting nature.

Some client goals reflect the level of their own disturbance and are not in their healthy self-interest. Thus, counsellors need to be sceptical while discussing goals with clients and should not take an overly consumeristic approach to goal setting. A typical example of a goal that is based on the client's level of disturbance and is not in the long-term interest of the client is the anorectic's goal of losing more weight.

My final point with respect to client goals concerns how explicit to make the discussion of such goals. I mentioned earlier that it is possible for client and counsellor to agree implicitly on the client's goals. However, in such circumstances there is the danger that the more implicit the agreement, the greater the scope for misunderstanding and error.

8. Vary the use of structuring

Structure in counselling varies from the very unstructured, where the counsellor does not attempt to influence the course of sessions at all, to the very structured, where the counsellor has every minute accounted for and has his own agenda which excludes any items the client might wish to discuss. In my opinion, both extremes need to be avoided. Different clients benefit from different degrees of structuring. For example, some clients, who are hysterically organised in their personality and are disorganised in their attempts to make sense of their experiences, benefit from a structured approach to counselling, while others who are obsessionally organised in their personality, require less structure in counselling sessions. In the latter case decreasing structure needs to be introduced gradually, since these clients are quite intolerant of experiences that are loosely organised.

Convention in counselling has it that sessions are 50 minutes long, enabling the counsellor to have a 10 minute break between clients. However, there is nothing sacred about the 50 minute hour and, under some circumstances, variations in this convention is essential. Sometimes, for example in dealing with certain post-traumatic stress disorders, the 50 minute hour is insufficient if the client is repeatedly to process her traumatic experience in a way that enables her to integrate it into her meaning structure. In these circumstances, counsellors need to set aside anything up to four hours in order to deal with the situation.

For other clients, and here I am thinking of those whose attention span and ability to comprehend is limited, 50 minutes is far too long and sessions lasting for 15 or 20 minutes are much more productive. Here, as elsewhere, it is important for counsellors to avoid rigidity and to be flexible.

While I advocate flexibility within counselling sessions, I do not advocate that counsellors violate the healthy boundaries that need to surround the counselling process. For example, if at the end of a session a client says: 'I think we need to continue this. Why don't we meet over dinner', warning bells should ring loudly for the counsellor. However, in the literature there are a number of accounts which demonstrate that important turning points in the counselling relationship occurred when the counsellor responded to a client's invitation to meet outside the counselling session – perhaps to go home and meet the client's family. I realise that I am now entering a veritable minefield. While my own position is that healthy boundaries are those that are generally adhered to rigidly, such boundaries are to be avoided. Needless to say, any changes in normal practice concerning such boundaries do need to be explored carefully with counselling supervisors.

9. Work with one problematic theme at a time

It is usual for clients to seek counselling for several problems which may be based on a small number of underlying themes. While it is important to respect the complexity of a client's problems, it is also important to work with these problems in a way in which they can be solved.

Normally this means dealing with one client problem or theme at a time. It is important for counsellors to avoid trying to solve all the clients problems at once. If they try to do this they are in the same situation as the man in the circus who attempts to keep a large number of spinning plates going all at once; eventually he gets tired and the plates come crashing to the ground. Thus, it is important for counsellors to work with one focus at a time, by which I mean a client issue that has a discernible theme. Sometimes this cannot be done since changes in the client's life circumstances preclude this thematic focus. Once again, counsellors need to be flexible; they should stay with a particular theme, when this is indicated, and work on a problem with which the client is currently preoccupied when it is more productive to do so.

10. Vary counselling from a narrow focus to a comprehensive focus from client to client

Psychodynamic counsellors are very much concerned with in-depth counselling and criticise their non-psychodynamic colleagues for not working deeply enough with client material. In this point, I am concerned with the question of breadth; namely, are counsellors working broadly enough (rather than deeply enough) with their clients?

There are some clients who seek help for a particular problem and do not wish to discuss any other issue in their lives. For such clients, narrow-focused counselling is called for. Although many counsellors may wish to broaden the counselling, this should be resisted because these clients are just not interested in doing so. Other clients, however, have problems in large areas of their personal functioning. They may have problems in the areas of behaviour, affect, sensation, imagery, cognition and are also experiencing problems in their interpersonal relationships and their biological functioning. I am referring here to the seven modalities of human experience that Arnold Lazarus (1981) argues a counsellor needs to be sensitive to when working with clients.

Counsellors need to be aware, then, that their work is going to vary from a narrow focus to a broad, comprehensive focus from client to client. With some clients, counsellors may start out with a narrow focus and the client may later become aware of other problems in her life. The work then will become more comprehensive. However, this shift from the narrow to the comprehensive does not inevitably occur as counselling proceeds, and counsellors should resist the temptation to broaden the work with clients when this is not indicated.

11. Be flexible using within-session and between-session foci
Some counsellors, particularly those who adhere to the Kleinian school of psychodynamic psychotherapy, believe that almost every word uttered by the client refers to some unconscious aspect of his relationship with the counsellor. I call this process 'hothousing', in that the exploration between client and counsellor becomes focused on the suffocating aspects of their relationship. Other counsellors believe that they have very little stimulus value for their clients. The entire thrust of their work with their clients is focused on the clients' outside life and contains little if any reference to the developing relationship between them. I call this 'coldhousing', in that the relationship between counsellor and client is, as it were, put into cold storage.

It is often stated by counsellors that seeing a client weekly involves 1 hour's contact out of a possible 168. The argument continues that, in order for counselling to make a difference for clients, counsellors need to encourage them to apply what they have learnt in the counselling room to their outside lives. However, one of the ways of ensuring that counselling makes a difference is for counsellors to deal with issues that emerge in the therapeutic relationship and which seem to parallel the problems that clients experience in their everyday lives. It is therefore important for counsellors to realise that clients differ concerning how much the focus of counselling needs to be placed on the here-and-now relationship, with all its historical ramifications for the client, and how much it needs to be placed on the there-and-now aspects of the client's life outside counselling. To assume that all clients need a there-and-now approach or a here-and-now approach is demonstrating again the type of black and white thinking that the field needs to avoid.

12. Ensure that counsellors and clients have a mutual understanding of relevant change-enhancing tasks and can use them suitably

A task in counselling is something that the counsellor or the client engages in. A task can refer to a specific activity such as a homework assignment; for example, the client agrees to spend 10 minutes a day keeping a 'feeling' diary. Alternatively, a task can refer to a more general activity such as self-exploration. Counselling tasks can occur within the session or between sessions. Needless to say, different counselling orientations advocate different tasks for both counsellor and client.

When considering tasks, it is important that clients (i) understand what they may have been asked to do; (ii) have sufficient competence to do it; and (iii) see the sense and relevance of doing it, i.e. understand that engaging in relevant task activity can help them to achieve their goals.

Three or four years ago an article appeared in *The Guardian* entitled 'Probationer did not understand Apple Therapy'. The client who was on probation, went to a day centre where he attended a group in which role playing was used. In one of the exercises the group leader encouraged him to play the role of a fruit, more specifically an apple. He absconded from the centre because, he claimed, this activity did not really get to the 'core' of his issues. By running away, we could say that he 'blew a raspberry' at the leader for asking him to engage in a meaningless task. This example rather neatly and humorously illustrates the importance of clients' understanding the relationship between what they are being asked to do and their counselling goals. Counsellors need to discuss their tasks openly and explicitly with their clients if they are to prevent their clients from being mystified as was the probationer.

When planning effective therapeutic tasks, counsellors need to take into account a number of important variables. They need to consider, among others, a client's personality, gender, race, world view, learning style and speed of learning. In addition, the possible therapeutic potency of the tasks needs to be appraised. For example, there are some therapeutic tasks that do not have sufficient potency to enable clients to achieve certain goals. Thus, a client can be asked to stand on her head and chant a mantra several times a day for many months, but doing so, in all probability, will not help her to get over her panic attacks.

Thus, counsellors need to become knowledgeable about the research literature in counselling in order to identify those tasks that are potent enough to help clients solve their problems. Too often, counselling is guided not by the client's problems but by the counsellor's predilections. This is reflected in an old joke: that if you go to a Freudian therapist you begin to dream in Freudian symbols; if you go to a Jungian you dream in Jungian symbols, and if you go to a behaviour therapist you don't dream at all!

13. Tailor the use of therapeutic interventions to the client's unique set of circumstances, interests, characteristics, learning style and other salient variables

By now it should be clear that I am a strong advocate of flexibility in counselling. The idea that all clients benefit from a single approach to counselling is one that goes against not only clinical sense, but also common sense. Individual differences between clients need to be respected and counsellors need to tailor their interventions accordingly.

There is some evidence that in certain British sub-cultures making links between past and present, disclosing one's problems to a stranger and exploring these problems are alien activities. Consequently, if a counsellor expects a client who comes from such a sub-culture to adjust to the counsellor's approach rather than vice-versa, it is likely that the counselling will stall quite quickly.

For example, if I were to go into therapy now, I would not work well with a counsellor who advocated the use of imagery interventions because I really do not have a vivid pictorial imagination and find working with symbols quite alien. In addition, I would not work well with a counsellor who has a decided spiritual orientation, since I am a dyed-in-the-wool atheist, and I would quickly become frustrated with a counsellor who is silent and quite passive in her interactive style. This personal example demonstrates, I hope, that different counsellors need to use different interventions with different clients.

Being aware of a client's understanding of language is particularly pertinent here, since effective counselling depends upon counsellor and client developing a shared language framework. I once encouraged one of my female clients to accept herself as a fallible human being and was taken aback when this produced a hostile response from her. 'What do you mean,' she said. 'I'm not that fat!' To her, 'fallible' meant obese!

When tailoring interventions, it is helpful for counsellors to know what interests their clients have so that they can use analogies that make sense to these clients. For example, I am quite interested in boxing and would resonate to a knowledgable analogy involving pugilism as its content; however, if a counsellor started using an opera analogy or one from the world of ballet, I would quickly turn off. Arnold Lazarus (1981) has said that counselling/psychotherapy is both an art and a science. Thus, scientific research might indicate that a particular counselling technique needs to be used with a particular client. However, how the counsellor employs the technique with due regard to voice tone, voice cadence, imagery and language can make a crucial difference to the success or failure of the intervention. Knowing the kind of language and the type of imagery that a client is likely to respond favourably to is part of mastering the art of counselling.

14. Adjust the pace of making interventions to the client's pace and style of processing information

It is important to adjust the pace of making counselling interventions to take into account the client's pace and style of processing information, among other learning variables.

One of the most influential figures on my career as a counsellor has been Albert Ellis, who is the founder of Rational Emotive Behaviour Therapy, an approach for which I am quite well known in this country. Every year I go over to America to find out the latest developments in REBT and to talk to Ellis about matters of theoretical and practical interest. Occasionally in the context of these discussions I talk to him about a personal concern. When I do this he intervenes quite quickly with me because he assumes that, as I understand REBT very well and can think as quickly as he can, I can process information as quickly as he comes up with it. I frequently have to tell him to slow down as I *cannot* process the information that quickly.

It is important, therefore, that counsellors adjust their pace of making interventions to enable their clients to process information fully. This will enable clients to get the most out of what the counsellor is saying. Some counsellors work well with quick thinking clients, but become impatient with clients who process information more slowly. Other counsellors prefer to work with the latter group and would struggle with clients who think very quickly on their feet.

Some clients tend to act first and process information later, while others prefer to chew matters over before they act. Given this, when counsellors work with these two different types of individual, they need to adjust their interventions accordingly. For example, encouraging the latter group to act before thinking things through thoroughly is likely to prove unproductive. It follows from this analysis that counsellors need to become aware of salient aspects of their clients' styles of learning and to pace their interventions accordingly.

15. Use the 'challenging, but not overwhelming' principle

It is my view that, when clients engage in tasks that are challenging for them, but not overwhelming, their progress in counselling is enhanced. As such, counselling needs to be neither too threatening and overwhelming on the one hand, nor too cosy and unchallenging on the other. It is the task of counsellors to encourage their clients to engage in tasks that pose a challenge, while at the same time to protect them from engaging in tasks that may be overwhelming for them at a given point in the counselling process. Many clients deprive themselves of making gains in counselling by waiting until they feel comfortable before doing something constructive, when in fact a sense of comfort comes from acting uncomfortably and does not predate such action. Thus, I frequently encourage my clients to do things unconfidently, uncomfortably and uncourageously if they want to become comfortable, confident and courageous. This of course involves their taking a risk and undertaking a challenging activity. There is, regrettably, no substitute for this, if clients are to make progress.

III
Improvements in Identifying and Addressing Clients' Obstacles to Change

16. Be mindful of and guided by the client's stage of change
Prochaska and DiClemente (1984) have identified five stages of personal change. The first stage is called 'Pre-contemplative' and describes a situation where a client has yet to decide that he has a problem that he wishes to change. Such clients are referred by outside agencies such as the courts or feel compelled to attend counselling, for example by a partner; however, they do not consider that they have a problem. The second stage is called 'Contemplative'. At this point the client has begun to recognise that he does have a problem that he may wish to change and is exploring the nature of his concerns. The third stage involves 'Decision-making'; the client does now recognise that he has a problem and decides to do something about it. The fourth stage is the 'Action' stage of change, where the client is ready to act to overcome his problem and to work towards achieving his goals. The final stage of change is called 'Maintenance'. The client has made progress and needs to maintain these gains; if he does not do so, relapse is likely to occur.

The important implication of this model is that it is necessary for a counsellor to use interventions that are suitable for the stage of change that the client is in. For example, when a client is ready to act to overcome his problems, an intervention more suited to the contemplative stage of change is inappropriate. On the other hand, a counsellor who encourages action when a client is in either the pre-contemplative or contemplative stages of change is likely to engender resistance. Thus, it is crucial to tailor counselling interventions according to the stage of change that clients are at.

17. Discover the client's past attempts at solving problems and create distance between these strategies and what the counsellor will be offering
It is frequently helpful to ask clients questions about their previous attempts to cope with their problems. It is also useful to find out what informal and formal sources of help they have sought prior to seeking counselling and what the outcome of these endeavours were. In exploring this issue, it is important that counsellors discover not only what clients

have done that has not proven helpful to them, but also strategies that have been helpful to them, so that the counsellor can avoid the former and build on the latter.

When the counsellor has identified previously ineffective strategies, it is important to create a distance between these strategies and the interventions that the counsellor intends to use. Since individuals find it easy to keep using ineffective strategies, part of the work of the counsellor is to help the client to realise the ineffective nature of such strategies and to encourage him to try something different.

18. Discover and deal with client's obstacles to change at each point in the counselling process

Obstacles to client change can occur throughout the counselling process. Thus, at the outset clients may come into counselling harbouring certain fears about the counselling process. For example, some clients fear that the counsellor is going to take away their autonomy or encourage them to become dependent on the counselling process. In such situations, it is important for counsellors to identify such fears and help to dispel them.

In the middle phase of counselling, the full implications of personal change have often become apparent and clients will have become aware of what they may have to give up in order to overcome their problems. Thus, clients may realise, albeit implicitly, that if they are to change they will lose any secondary gains that they have derived from their problems. Thus, they may lose a sense of familiarity that is experienced because they have lived with their problems for a long period of time. They may also lose a related sense of identity if they overcome their problems. Here, it is important for counsellors to help their clients recognise that there are both gains and losses that occur when striving towards personal change, and also to encourage them to accept that this is a natural aspect of such change.

At the end phase of counselling, obstacles to leaving counselling tend to surface. Questions such as 'Can I cope on my own?' need to be addressed. Clients need to be helped to realise that, not only have they benefited from the work they have done in counselling, but they have also internalised a way of helping themselves which they can utilise without the presence of the counsellor.

In addition, at the end phase of counselling, clients' ambivalences about ending relationships in general tend to surface. Bringing the counselling process to a suitable end not only serves to encourage clients to cope on their own, but also serves as a healthy model for ending relationships and moving on.

19.Monitor and learn from things left unsaid
Regan and Hill (1992) discovered that both clients and counsellors are able to identify a range of experiences which they have during counselling sessions, but which they do not articulate in these sessions. I am not suggesting here that counsellors compulsively encourage their clients to articulate all of their experiences, nor that they disclose all of their own experiences. I do suggest, however, that counsellors are aware that clients do not disclose certain aspects of their experiences during counselling (both about the nature of their problems and about the counselling process itself) and that they need to help clients to talk about those aspects of their unexpressed experiences that it is useful to explore. There are two ways of doing this: first, to refer the issue to the reflection process mentioned earlier, and second, to deal with it in a structured formal review session.

Counsellors may need to make sense of their own unexpressed experiences during the counselling process. One good way do this is to tape-record counselling sessions and to play them back periodically in order to identify their unexpressed experiences. These can be discussed with supervisors and decisions can be made concerning how they need to be dealt with in the counselling relationship.

20. Attend to and learn from one's own feeling reactions to clients and use this learning accordingly
This issue is emphasised by psychodynamic counsellors and points to the fact that one fruitful source of learning about one's clients is from one's own emotional responses to them. These are called counter-transference reactions in the literature. The value of using one's own feeling reactions to clients as a guide for learning about the possible interpersonal impact that clients have upon others rests on the extent to which counsellors can rely on their feeling responses as accurate, undistorted sources of evidence. It is for this reason that counsellors are frequently encouraged to have personal therapy, so that they can explore their own emotional sensitivities and become aware of possible distortions in their counter-transference reactions.

While there is much research which shows that counsellors value their personal therapy (e.g. Norcross, Dryden & Di Michele, 1992) it remains to be shown that having personal therapy leads counsellors to become more effective practitioners, and little is known of its effect on the way counter-transference reactions are used in the counselling process. Nevertheless, counsellors from all orientations need to attend to their own reactions as a valuable source of learning about their clients, and they need to be trained explicitly how best to do this.

IV
Making Improvements in Helping Clients to Consolidate their Gains in Counselling

21. Understand and capitalise on client change; attribute change to clients and empower them

I want to emphasise here how important it is for counsellors to understand client change as it occurs. In particular, this involves discovering from clients which psychological processes they have modified. By so doing, counsellors can encourage their clients to learn from their own change processes and to capitalise on this learning.

As such, it is important to explore with clients whether the gains they have made can be explained by modifications in their own psychological processes or by the occurrence of fortuitous changes in their physical or interpersonal environment which are outside of their control.

When counsellors discover that change has been effected by clients themselves, it is important to help clients to attribute such changes explicitly to their own efforts. Counsellors should not take the major credit for client change. Thus, when a client says to a counsellor 'You have helped me enormously. Without you I could not have achieved so much', it is important for the counsellor to remind the client that, while the counsellor's input may have been important, it is the client herself who has derived benefit from the counselling process by putting into practice in her everyday life what she has learnt from the counselling process

When it is apparent that a client has improved without effecting any changes in her psychological processes, it is important for the counsellor to encourage her to acknowledge this. Then, it is important to explore with her how she could have effected change in herself even if the adverse circumstances which have now changed for the better still existed.

22. Encourage clients to generalise their learning

This point follows naturally on from the previous one. Once clients have attributed change to their own efforts and understood how they brought about such change, it is important for counsellors to help them to consolidate this learning and to generalise it. It is important to recognise, then, that, if counsellors want clients to generalise their learning, they need to plan for it to happen. In short, generalisation should not be taken for granted. For example, if a client is dealing productively with a conflict that he has been having with a female co-worker and understands how he is changing, it should not be expected that he will, as a matter of course, generalise this learning to dealing more constructively with similar women in other settings. Indeed, it frequently happens in counselling that clients express surprise that they can generalise their learning from one situation to another. Therefore, counsellors who place this issue firmly on the counselling agenda at an appropriate time will help their clients more effectively than counsellors who wait for clients to bring up the issue of generalisation.

23. Anticipate and address relapse

Counsellors who work in the addiction field know only too well that relapse frequently occurs. Consequently, there has been a great deal of interest in this field in what is called 'relapse prevention'. Anybody who has tried to give up smoking or remain on a calorie-controlled diet will know what I mean when I say that relapses frequently occur in behaviour change. As Mark Twain said about smoking, 'Giving up smoking is easy. I have done it thousands of times!' However, it is important to recognise that so-called relapses occur in all areas of life, not only in the addictions. When anticipating any kind of relapse, it is important for counsellors to convey to clients that this is a natural process in human change and yet one where they can exercise some control.

Relapse prevention involves clients' (i) identifying vulnerable situations in which relapses may occur; (ii) identifying relevant psychological processes (such as black and white thinking) that may promote relapse, and (iii) constructing, practising, maintaining and generalising a variety of coping strategies to ensure that relapses do not occur or if they do that their onset may serve as a cue for productive problem-solving rather than as a cue for reinstatement and continuation of the previously entrenched self-defeating behaviour.

24. Encourage clients to become their own counsellors

In my view, it is insufficient for counsellors to help clients to identify and deal with their problems. Additionally, it is important for counsellors to help clients to internalise a way of helping themselves in the future so that they do not become dependent on counselling. In the world of psychology much is made of the importance of 'giving psychology away'. Along with other counselling authorities such as Robert Carkhuff and Richard Nelson-Jones, I advocate 'give counselling away' in that we should deliberately train clients in self-helping skills. This will most frequently take place during the late phase of the counselling process, and it is likely to occur at a time when clients are seeking to leave counselling because they have derived benefit from the process. However, if counsellors give their clients an adequate rationale for a period of deliberate self-help skills training, clients will often see the sense of this and will opt for it. This will ensure that clients get the most from counselling.

25. Prepare for ending and use follow-up sessions

Many counsellors believe that implicit in many client problems is a difficulty in ending relationships. If this is correct, then it follows that counsellors need to help clients deal explicitly with the end of the counselling relationship.

As a client, my own experience of therapists helping me deal with the end of therapy has been mixed. One carefully helped me to prepare for its end, while another abruptly announced that the current session was to be our last. So I know how difficult it is to deal with poorly managed endings. Some proponents of brief psychodynamic counselling argue that it is important to prepare for the ending of the counselling process right at its beginning.

Having said this, in my experience, clients differ quite markedly concerning their attitudes towards the ending of counselling. Some are prepared to stop quite abruptly – at their own behest, I might add – while others require quite a long period of preparation for, and grieving over the loss of, what has been for them an important relationship.

The two main ways of ending that seem to be favoured by most counsellors concern (i) the setting of an ending date with no change in the frequency of sessions and (ii) a gradual increase in time between sessions with the final session decided upon during this winding down process. Here counselling sessions may move from being held weekly to being held fortnightly, then monthly and so on. In my own experience, when I have outlined these two ways of ending to clients (i.e. when we have begun to talk about endings), I am quite happy for them to choose whichever method of ending seems to be most helpful to them.

In addition, the issue of follow-up sessions needs to be considered by counsellors. If counsellors are to evaluate their work properly, they need to measure not only the immediate outcome of their work with particular clients, but also the durability of such outcomes. This can be done by holding periodic follow-up sessions which might take place face-to-face or, if a client lives a long distance from the counsellor, over the telephone. The purposes of follow-up sessions are (i) to determine the extent to which the client has maintained the gains that she has derived from counselling and (ii) to deal with any issues that may be preventing them from maintaining their gains. If serious obstacles to maintenance of client gain are discovered, or, indeed, if the client has deteriorated, then counsellor and client need to discuss the possible resumption of counselling for an agreed (perhaps brief) period.

V
Improvements in Professional Knowledge and Self-Reflection

26. Use questionnaires and inventories for a variety of purposes

There is a myriad of useful questionnaires and inventories in the counselling literature that can be used for the purposes of helping counsellors and clients to (i) clarify clients' issues, (ii) stimulate the work of counselling, and (iii) evaluate that work. It is my view that counsellors tend to see the use of such questionnaires and inventories as mechanistic and somewhat de-humanising. I believe this is an unfortunate view. Such questionnaires can be introduced into the counselling process in a way that is in keeping with the basic philosophy of counselling, i.e. of demonstrating respect for clients. If a rationale for their use is carefully explained and clients are given the option not to complete them, I cannot honestly see any realistic objection to their employment. I use questionnaires that assess (i) clients' opinions about the cause of their problems and what may constitute the most effective approach to these problems, (ii) the stage of change that clients are in, and (iii) clients' underlying belief systems. I also make regular use of Lazarus and of Lazarus's (1991) Life History Inventory, which gives a broad picture of the clients' past and present functioning.

So I would urge counsellors to reconsider their views on the use of such questionnaires, since in my experience they can enhance rather than impede the counselling process and can be used in a way that respects clients and protects their autonomy.

27. Utilise research findings

In 1980 I published an article encouraging counsellors to make use of the counselling research literature (Dryden, 1980). I wrote this paper when a survey of the membership of BAC that was conducted in the late 1970s indicated that counselling research was the least important priority with which the organisation should be concerned (Nelson-Jones & Coxhead, 1978). The current picture is slightly more favourable to research, but not that much. While BAC has a sub-committee on research, it still seems to me that most counsellors do not see the relevance of research findings or are frightened of counselling research since research papers are often written in a complex manner. It is the case that counsellors frequently encourage their clients to enter into zones of discomfort to confront what they find frightening. Thus, I urge counsellors to do the same with respect to counselling research. When they do so, it is important for them to read research literature critically. For example, when reading up on research on college students, it is important to question the relevance of the findings for other client populations.

Indeed, having a sceptical, research-orientated perspective on counselling would lead counsellors to be wary of the extravagant claims made in some quarters for the quickness of 'cures'. Doing so would mean that research evidence would be requested to support such claims before one parted with not inconsiderable amounts of money to be trained in such 'magical techniques'.

However, if counsellors do not keep up to date with the research literature on counselling, then they are going to be ignorant of modern developments in the treatment of, for example, panic disorder and post traumatic stress disorder.

28. Develop an informed and disciplined eclectic and integrative approach (including when not to be eclectic)

This point is particularly salient after counsellors have been trained professionally and have obtained a lot of counselling experience. Eclecticism in counselling means having a particular theoretical approach to the work and using diverse sources, systems and styles borrowed from other approaches, but in a way that is consistent with one's theoretical approach. Integration, on the other hand, involves not only drawing from a diverse range of therapeutic approaches but also integrating these at a theoretical level. Eclecticism and integration in counselling and psychotherapy are becoming more popular as people come to see the limitations of specific orientations. While I applaud and advocate this development, I am beginning to be concerned that it is not being appreciated that moving towards an eclectic or an integrative mode of practice is an activity that depends upon a thorough grounding in training and experience. Whenever I increasingly encounter counselling trainees who claim to be eclectic or integrative without having such solid foundations on which to draw, I sigh inwardly and express doubt about their claims.

Having said this, the movement towards eclecticism and integration involves the breakdown of rigid barriers between practitioners of differing approaches and promotes a healthy dialogue among workers from diverse schools. As such it is to be welcomed.

However, a note of caution is in order here. We need to ask whether integrative or eclectic approaches to counselling are in fact more effective than specific approaches. Indeed, it is likely that under specific circumstances such specific approaches may well be more effective than eclectic or integrative approaches In this vein, there is research that indicates that a standard approach to simple phobias is more effective than a more eclectic (tailor-made) approach to this particular problem (Schulte et al., 1992). The sceptical but informed counsellor needs to ask under what circumstances are specific non-eclectic, non-tailor-made approaches more useful than bespoke approaches to the same problem.

29. Develop a counselling profile

As counsellors gain more experience and develop their skills, it is important for them to monitor their strengths and weaknesses. Thus, I suggest that, no matter how experienced or well trained a counsellor is, he would be wise to develop what I call a counselling profile to keep an ongoing record of these strengths and weaknesses. So many counsellors, in my experience, do not do this. Thus, they attend supervision and further training sessions but tend to forget what they have learnt in such sessions, with the result that they repeatedly make the same mistakes. Even though I applaud the emerging trend in counselling towards continuing professional education, without an ongoing record of one's strengths and weaknesses to act as a spur for further development, this trend may be an empty exercise of collecting CPE hours rather than furthering expertise.

30. Supervise yourself and also seek supervision from others

It is a commendable that in Britain ongoing supervision of one's work as a counsellor is deemed to be required activity no matter how experienced one is. Supervision can occur in many different modes, from individual and group supervision to peer supervision. However, it is also important for counsellors to supervise themselves and not to rely solely on help from others.

I encourage counsellors to continue to audiotape their counselling sessions and listen periodically to randomly selected sessions. Using one of a number of self-supervision inventories, counsellors can gain a lot from listening to themselves and from supervising themselves on their work. I wish to stress that I do not regard self-supervision as a replacement for supervision from others. Rather, I argue that the two activities complement each other.

Conclusion

Counselling is a dynamic professional activity in which improvements in theory and practice continue to be made as the profession develops. Consequently, the thirty improvements suggested here should be regarded as interim suggestions and should themselves be subject to improvement.

References

Dryden, W. (1980). The relevance of research in counselling and psychotherapy for the counselling practitioner. *British Journal of Guidance and Counselling*, 8 (2), 224-232.

Lazarus, A.A. (1981). *The practice of multimodal therapy.* New York: McGraw-Hill.

Miller, D.J., & Thelen, M.H. (1986). Knowledge and beliefs about confidentiality in psychotherapy. *Professional Psychology: Research and Practice,* 17, 15-19.

Nelson-Jones, R., & Coxhead, P. (1978). Whither BAC: a survey of members' views on policy and practices. *Counselling News,* 21, 2-5.

Norcross, J.C., Dryden, W., & DiMichele, J.T. (1992). British clinical psychologists, III: What's good for the goose? *Clinical Psychology Forum,* 44, 29-33.

Prochaska, J.O., & DiClemente, C.C. (1964). *The transtheoretical approach: crossing the traditional boundaries of therapy.* Homewood, IL: Dow Jones-Irwin.

Regan, A.M., & Hill, C.E. (1992). Investigation of what clients and counselors do not say in brief therapy. *Journal of Counselling Psychology,* 39, 168-174.

Schulte, D., Kunzel, R., Pepping, G., & Schulte-Bahrenberg, T. (1992). Tailor-made versus standardised therapy of phobic patients. *Advances in Behaviour Research and Therapy,* 14, 67-92.

Strean, H.S. (1959). The use of the patient as consultant. *Psychoanalysis and Psychoanalytic Review,* 46 (2), 36-44.

2

keeping the door open: the need for counselling in a complex, ever-changing world

I gave this paper at Eastbourne Town Hall on June 11, 1997. I had previously read in the Eastbourne Herald that Open Door in Eastbourne would have to cease offering a counselling service due to a significant reduction in its funding. Since Eastbourne is now my second home, I wanted to make a tangible contribution to Open Door's plight. This paper was the result and it raised £1500 which, I am very pleased to report, helped to save Open Door's counselling service; at least for another year.

I was not sure who would attend my lecture so I decided to deliver a paper for the general public.

When I read in the Eastbourne Herald that the existence of the counselling service offered by Open Door was threatened due to lack of funding, I experienced a strong desire to do something to help. This lecture is the product of this strong desire.

The field of counselling has experienced tremendous growth in the last fifteen years. Agony aunts and uncles regularly advise their correspondents and readers to seek counselling for a whole range of problems. Soap opera characters are increasingly seen going to consult a counsellor, and counselling training courses from introductory to Masters level are proliferating like rabbits on heat. But perhaps the most telling sign that counselling is no longer a fringe activity is that it is increasingly being attacked and criticised both from within the field and from without. When counselling and therapy was for the few it could be safely ignored. Now that it is a form of help to which people are increasingly turning, it can no longer be ignored and is therefore a target for criticism. I don't think that the field should be at all threatened by the critiques of counselling that now appear, even if some of the critics are sadly misinformed and show a shockingly prejudiced view of those who seek counselling. Clients are portrayed either as self-indulgent people with too much time on their hands and too much money in their pockets, or as weak, spineless, dependent individuals who flock to the inner sanctum of the counselling confessional at the drop of an emotional hat.

Since I passionately believe in free speech, I welcome these critics of counselling. We in the field have the freedom to respond as we see fit, and even if the criticisms receive more space or airtime than the responses, this is the way of the world. The field of counselling has no right to receive special treatment. As a tender-minded profession, we have to live in what is increasingly a tough-minded world. Counsellors face the challenge of marrying our traditional tender-minded attitudes with the tough-minded attitudes of a sceptical, cost-effective society if we are to work effectively within this society. This does not mean that we should stop trying to make the world a more tender-minded place in which to live – far from it. However, if we ignore that world and its developing attitudes, we will eventually return to being a fringe activity.

What does this mean for voluntary-aided counselling agencies? It means that they will have to make the case for funding counselling services and to compete aggressively with other equally deserving agencies for a share of dwindling resources. In short, such services will have to dig in and fight. I am particularly pleased to help Open Door in its particular fight and to have the opportunity to talk about how the field of counselling can survive, and indeed thrive, well into the next millennium by marrying its traditional tender-minded strengths with tough-minded qualities. Doing so will, in my view, make counselling a more well-rounded profession.

Traditional tender-minded counselling qualities

Let me begin my discussion by reviewing counselling's tender-minded core. Although there are many different counselling approaches (see Dryden, 1996), most counsellors share some common ideas. The first of these ideas concerns the therapeutic value of talking. When people are confused, they tend to toss these confused ideas around in their heads in a way that often results in increased confusion and stress. Being able to externalise their confusion in words often leads to a decrease in tension and an emerging clarity, particularly if the person listening allows this process to occur and does not cut the person off with well-meaning phrases which serve only to curb self-exploration.

Critics of counselling claim with some truth that friends and relatives can offer this listening ear and thus make counsellors redundant. The bit that is true in this critique is that if we are lucky we may have friends and relatives who can offer a non-intrusive listening ear. However, more often than not our friends and relatives find it difficult to tolerate our distress. They try to help us to feel better by saying things such as: 'Don't cry, it will all turn out for the best', or 'We all feel like that at one time or another'. If we are less fortunate we may hear: 'Pull yourself together'; 'Don't be silly', or even 'What's wrong with you?' It is an indictment of present society that, while we are making stupendous advances in the field of technology, we still find it enormously difficult to listen to one another with compassion and empathy.

One of the central skills that trained counsellors bring to the process of counselling is the ability to provide a climate where clients can put into words their inner distress and confusion. As I said earlier, being able to do this is therapeutic in itself, and many clients require nothing more than to be allowed to explore themselves in their own way. Exactly forty years ago, in a seminal article on counselling, Carl Rogers (1957) argued that, if counsellors genuinely show their clients an attitude of respect and if they communicate to their clients an accurate understanding of what their clients are expressing, then they will help their clients to deepen their ability to explore their concerns in a way that results in greater clarity about their inner experiences.

When a person tries to communicate her inner experiences to another person and this person either cuts off this process or responds in a way that deepens the other's shame, one of three things may happen. First, the person in distress may retreat within herself. She may keep her feelings *to* herself and sometimes *from* herself, with the result that her distress is intensified and a sense of hopelessness about herself and about her ability to resolve her problems is engendered. Second, the person may externalise her distress and act in ways that society labels as anti-social. Such is the nature of this 'anti-social' behaviour that people see only the overt behaviour and not the inner concealed distress that has occasioned it. Third, the person may attempt to deal with her distress by resorting to abusing substances of one sort or another. This inevitably creates a second problem – that stemming from a dependent reliance on the substance which, even if resolved, will leave the person with her original problem unresolved. The irony is that society pays more in financial terms to clear up the mess caused, in part, by its failure to provide such people with early effective counselling than it will ever pay for providing such counselling in the first place.

I have stressed that all many clients require is a safe, non-intrusive therapeutic place where they can explore themselves in the presence of a well-intentioned person who can offer empathy and allow them to explore their confused feelings and experiences. Sadly, however, numerous clients require more than this, and this is where friends and family get completely out of their depth. The second idea that I want to discuss within counselling's tender-minded core, then, concerns the importance of offering clients a framework within which they can develop a coherent and personally meaningful way of understanding themselves and their experiences. Different counselling approaches offer clients different frameworks, and perhaps the most important ingredient here is that the counsellor offers the client a framework for understanding himself which makes sense to him and which he can use as a springboard for personal change. If this is not the case, then the client may not be helped to go beyond the benefits of exploring himself and having his explorations understood and accepted. Depending on her therapeutic approach, either the counsellor may formally introduce this framework to the client, or it may be introduced more implicitly and become apparent in the counsellor's interventions. In my own approach to counselling, known as Rational Emotive Behaviour Therapy, I introduce this framework in an explicit manner since I believe that doing so helps the client to decide whether or not he wants to go beyond what he has achieved from being allowed to explore himself in an open-ended manner. However, my psychodynamic colleagues, for example, do not do this, since they believe that a formal exposition of the psychodynamic framework is neither necessary nor helpful to the client. Their framework is therefore implicit in the way they respond to their clients.

I want to stress here that this second idea usually becomes salient after the client has experienced a relationship with his counsellor based on the principles that I outlined when discussing the first idea, i.e. the importance of being heard and being allowed to explore oneself in one's own way. Indeed, if the client has not been allowed this period of unfettered self-exploration, he is likely to experience this framework for understanding himself either as a set of interesting ideas which he cannot directly relate to his own experience or as something imposed on him at a time when he is unable to digest it.

The third idea that is part of the tender-minded core of counselling concerns the importance of the client using this new understanding to promote change. If this is not done, then the client will not integrate it into his life in a way that makes a difference. When this is not done, the client experiences his new understanding as intellectual rather than emotional. He will say things like 'I understand it in my head but not in my gut.' For new understanding to make a difference to the client's life, it has to be acted on, and acted on repeatedly. This is the stage of counselling that is called *working through*. Counsellors differ in how much they leave this to chance. My own approach is to encourage clients to act on their new understanding in a structured way in the form of homework assignments, but this practice is by no means common practice in counselling.

The title of this talk contains the phrase 'in a complex, ever-changing world'. While humans vary in how we respond to change, it is a feature of our species that we do not readily embrace it. We value familiarity and tend to resist attempts to bring about change, often seeing it as change for the worse rather than change for the better. I mention in passing that there was more passionate reaction against plans to build a refreshment kiosk on the promenade beneath Meads than there was when the threat to the Open Door counselling service was announced! But we face much more threatening changes than tea kiosks, even though they are less discernible.

Here is a brief resumé of old certainties that we can no longer take for granted. We can no longer take for granted that we can be secure in our chosen job or occupation. Here, we face the breakdown of employment security resulting from increasing technological advances. We can no longer take for granted that our children and grandchildren or even we ourselves will live together in the sanctity of marriage. Divorce rates are rising and marriage is no longer generally accepted as an inevitable consummation of a committed relationships. We can no longer accept without question that men will do 'men's' work and women will do 'women's' work. Here we face the breakdown of gender-specific occupations and roles, and we enter an area where boys can no longer be expected to be boys and where sugar and the Spice girls are not invariably nice!

I mentioned technology in the above statement. The other day one of my clients mentioned that a few years ago when he went to work he began the day by opening his mail. Now, he has to open his mail, listen to the messages on his answer machine, deal with his e-mail and check his voice mail. He may be fortunate to have a job, but he, like tens of thousands of others and the figure will soon run into the millions, is being bombarded from all sides by the products of our technological ingenuity.

My purpose here is not to argue for or against these developments, but to note the impact that these changes will have on the human mind. This impact is not direct, but is mediated by the beliefs that we hold about ourselves, others and the world around us. My view is that the more rigid these beliefs are, the more we will disturb ourselves in the face of the breakdown of old certainties. The more we base our self-esteem on things like having a job or marriage, for example, the more vulnerable we will be to emotional disturbance if these once accepted givens are threatened. Counselling cannot reverse this trend towards increasing complexity and change, nor should it try to do so. But it can help us develop a set of flexible beliefs to cope with an increasingly flexible world. Black and white beliefs may have been sufficient when things were black and white, but they won't help us to adapt productively and thrive in a post-modern world dominated by shades of grey.

If counselling cannot and should not hold up the force of change, what can it do? Counselling can help people to explore their feelings about threats to the expected order; it can then help them to use a framework that will enable them to re-evaluate themselves and their experiences in the light of increasing complexity and change; and it can help them to use this understanding in their everyday lives.

To achieve this, counselling itself will have to first survive and then thrive in this same complex and ever-changing world. How can the field of counselling do this? First, it will have to engage in a period of self-exploration. Then it will have to develop a new understanding of itself in the context of this world, and finally, it will have to act on this understanding. In short, counselling will have to seek counselling! Unfortunately, I do not have the time tonight to counsel counselling. I will, however, outline my views of what counselling has to learn in order to survive and thrive in the new millennium. In brief, it will have to develop some tough-minded practices and marry these with its tender-minded philosophy.

Counselling and tough-minded practices
Evaluation
We live in a climate in which people demand that services give good value for money. Thus, rail services have to provide evidence that a large majority of trains run on time, and health trusts have to provide evidence that they are cutting waiting lists. It doesn't seem to matter that the trains are filthy and the toilets don't work, and it doesn't seem to matter that once you get into hospital the food is unpalatable and the nurses are too busy to be concerned that you are in pain. In this evaluation

and audit culture, what matters is what you can count rather than what you can feel. The irony here is that the buzzword of this culture is 'quality', and that is perhaps the one thing that does not seem to count when you strip away the fancy language and listen to the accounts of people's painful experiences of these services.

What this means for counselling is that we will increasingly be asked to prove that our services work and we will have to prove this in ways that the field is not generally comfortable with. For the field of counselling is concerned with such elusive things as the quality of the counselling relationship and what the client 'feels' that she has derived from counselling. Frankly, this won't wash with people who have control over the purse-strings. They want to know that counselling results in a measurable reduction in suffering, that our clients are being helped to get back to 'normal' in ways that can be quantified. This means that before and after counselling we will have to give our clients valid and reliable questionnaires that measure symptoms of depression, anxiety and other psychological problems. This is going to cause a lot of soul-searching among counsellors, many of whom have a basic distrust of such questionnaires, thinking that they objectify the client and introduce an unwarranted mechanistic attitude into the counselling process. However much counsellors find this approach to their work distasteful, my view is that they are going have to bite the bullet and prove to the satisfaction of other more tough-minded people that counselling works.

Managed care

There is another spectre on the horizon which will cause even more consternation among counsellors. Its name is 'managed care'. Remember the name of this spectre, for you will hear a lot more of it in the future. The concept of managed care originated in North America, where much health care is private and costs are largely borne by insurance companies. Now insurance companies are not known for their generosity or for their caring, despite what their glossy brochures say. They are interested primarily in making money, and they do this in two ways: first, by encouraging people to take out private insurance policies, and second, by restricting the amount of money that they pay out. By and large, they do this legally.

In the world of private psychiatric health care in North America, someone hit on the brilliant idea that this care had to be managed. Previously, care was in the hands of the practitioners and insurance companies paid out according to what the practitioners thought their clients needed. You might think that this is a sensible way of going about things. However, it was a recipe for disaster for the insurance companies, since they were footing the spiralling bill and they realised that they would soon lose their huge profits if this situation was allowed to continue. So they decided to take over the business of managing care. Practitioners in North America now have to specify a psychiatric diagnosis for their clients and are told by the insurance company how many therapy sessions they will be paid for. If they think that their clients need more sessions, they have to wrangle with the insurance company. The effect that managed care has had is to restrict long-term therapy and to lead to a burgeoning interest in brief therapy among therapists as they realise that will be reimbursed only for brief work.

Now you may think that this situation will not happen here, but you would be wrong. It has already arrived, at least in the private sphere. Increasingly in Britain, insurance companies are asking therapists to submit treatment plans and they will pay only for acute conditions. For 'acute' read 'brief'. Clients who have chronic psychiatric conditions will have to pay for longer-term therapy themselves. My guess is that it will not be long before managed care becomes the norm in NHS psychiatric and psychological clinics up and down the country. The mechanisms are already in place. NHS trusts already invite tenders for their services and so do GP fundholders. If you are a GP fundholder who are you going to employ – a consortium submitting a package based on managed care lines which will offer your patients a service at a reasonable price, or a consortium submitting a package where patients receive therapy managed by the therapists themselves which is costed at a far higher price?

What implication does all this have for Open Door? Let's suppose that it receives the money that it needs to run a proper counselling service. What is to stop another agency claiming that it can offer a service at a competitive price? It could happen, and if it does, and if Open Door wishes to compete in such a climate, then it will have to undercut other tenders. This will inevitably lead to clients receiving less counselling than they probably need. But if Open Door does not seek funding for its counselling service, as I am helping them to do now, then it may close and where will its clients go then? So in the near future I predict that agencies like Open Door will have to compete aggressively for resources. Let me repeat that phrase: 'compete aggressively for resources'. This is hardly the language of the tender-minded.

Marketing and lobbying
Over recent years we have seen numerous charitable groups employ marketing experts and lobbyists. The primary tasks of such people are basically to bring in money and to facilitate a change in the law so that the charities can offer their services to more and more people. This is an area where counsellors and psychotherapists have tended to lag behind, although there have been recent attempts by the United Kingdom

Council for Psychotherapy to lobby MPs in their attempt to set up a statutory register for psychotherapists. While counselling agencies like Open Door do not have the money to hire marketing and lobbying experts, they should, I believe try to persuade such people to give their services free of charge. Certain marketing companies, for example, like to demonstrate that they have a social conscience by offering their services gratis. It is their way of saying: 'We care'. A word of warning, though. Beneath their soft exterior these companies are hard-headed and will not give away their services to agencies who portray themselves in an overly tender-minded way. So even here, you will have to come across in a tough-minded manner.

Let me end with a story that I heard when I worked as a marriage guidance counsellor about fifteen years ago that captures the essence of marrying tough-minded and tender-minded attitudes. This was before the National Marriage Guidance Council changed its name to Relate. One of the counsellors who had worked in the service from the outset told us of a client whom she saw many years before. At the beginning of every counselling session, the client put half a crown down on the table. For those of you unfamiliar with the term 'half a crown', it is currently worth twelve and a half pence. If the client thought that the session was of value to her, she would leave the money on the table; however, if she thought that the session hadn't been of use to her, she would pick up the money and take it away with her. Perhaps this is the best way that counsellors can marry tender-minded and tough-minded attitudes – by offering the best possible service and encouraging the client to have the final say.

References

Dryden, W. (ed.) (1996). *Handbook of individual therapy*. London: Sage.

Rogers, C. R. (1957). The necessary and sufficient conditions for therapeutic personality change. *Journal of Consulting Psychology*, 21, 95-103.

3

why I no longer practise person-centred therapy and psychodynamic therapy: some personal reflections

I am currently Honourary Visiting Professor in the Psychology Department at the University of East London and giving occasional lectures to its students is a major duty of this post. I delivered this paper on April 25, 1997 to second year students on the MSc Counselling Psychology course.

In the lecture I wanted to show the students that one's initial training is but the first step in one's career as a counsellor and to invite them to reflect on the relationship between counselling orientation and the personality of the counsellor.

I first became interested in counselling and psychotherapy when I was doing a doctorate in social psychology at Bedford College, University of London in 1972. My thesis was on "Self-disclosure" and many of the references in this area related to counselling. During my reading, I decided that I wanted to pursue a career in counselling, and this decision prompted me to apply to be a volunteer for both the Samaritans and Nightline, the student telephone service. In the last year of my PhD, I took an introductory course in counselling at South West London College run by Brigid Proctor and her staff, which reinforced my decision to train professionally as a counsellor.

Early days: trainee counsellor at Aston University, 1974-5
In 1974 I applied for a place on the one-year, full-time Diploma in Counselling in Educational Settings course at Aston University in Birmingham. This was a person-centred course run by Richard Nelson -Jones and Donald Biggs, an American counselling psychologist who was seconded to the course for a year as a Fulbright fellow.

Initially I was very attracted to person-centred therapy because of its optimistic view of human beings. As is well known, Carl Rogers (1957), the founder of the approach, held that the person would inevitably move towards healthy personal development if she experienced the presence of certain core facilitative conditions when these conditions were offered by a significant person or persons in that individual's life. People sought counselling because they had not experienced the enduring presence of these conditions in their lives and had developed problems as a result. Many of these problems stemmed from a failure of clients to accept themselves and were reflected in disturbed emotions and self-defeating behaviour which were often manifest in their relationships with others.

From a person-centred perspective, the role of the counsellor is to develop a psychological contact with the client and to offer a safe environment in which the client can explore herself. The features of this safe interpersonal environment are the core facilitative conditions mentioned earlier: (i) empathy (the ability to sense and communicate an accurate understanding of the person's experiences from that person's point of view); (ii) unconditional positive regard (the genuine communication of an unconditional prizing of the client as that person is, not conditional on what she may become); and (iii) genuineness (the therapeutic communication of one's real feelings and reactions to the client and a congruence between one's feelings and one's behaviour in the counselling relationship). Genuineness entails the counsellor not hiding behind the facade of the role of counsellor, but involving the client in an honest, I–Thou encounter.

This latter condition resonated strongly with the research subject of my PhD thesis, self-disclosure. Sidney Jourard (1971), the father of self-disclosure research, had written that honest self-disclosure was a key feature of psychological health. This resonance led me to believe that I was on the right lines in my counsellor training and provided an important continuity between my academic interests and my emerging professional interests.

The view of the role of the counsellor as put forward by Rogers emphasised how important the counsellor was in the therapeutic process; for if the counsellor succeeded in communicating these core facilitative conditions to the client, and if the client experienced these counsellor-offered conditions, then the client's movement towards psychological health would be inevitable. Rogers's view, then, offered two important things to me as a trainee counsellor: a sense of importance, and a sense of being socially useful.

Looking back, it seems to me that I was desperately looking for these two qualities in my life. Although gaining a PhD was immensely important to me, it did not give me a sense of importance. I had only succeeded in achieving yet another academic degree, and I was aware even at that time that my research findings were far from earth-shattering, of interest perhaps to only a handful of self-disclosure researchers. Indeed, such was my disappointment about the likely impact of my research that I didn't even bother to write up my findings for publication. The idea that I could make such a powerful difference to the lives of my clients was a real attraction, and I couldn't wait to start practising.

In retrospect, it also seems that the promise of doing something socially useful was very appealing. I was very much aware of the pain of having psychological problems from first-hand experience (to which I will return later), and the idea of helping people to live more fulfilled lives fired me enthusiasm and desire. I could help myself as well as helping others. What bliss!

The first term at Aston involved trainees in intensive skills-based empathy training in which we counselled one another, had our interviews video-recorded, and analysed these interviews response by response in order to learn how to make more empathic responses. We also participated in a personal development group run by one of the university chaplains who was a trained TA therapist. And, of course, we made an intensive study of person-centred theory.

Looking back, it was an adequate preparation for seeing clients, but the course was not entirely internally consistent. The personal development group experience was inconsistent with the person-centred focus of the course, and there were signs that neither of the two trainers was thoroughly committed to the person-centred model. Indeed, 1974-5 marked the beginning of Richard Nelson-Jones' own journey towards a more integrative approach to counselling. Nevertheless, I 'felt', and was deemed, ready to see clients at the beginning of the second term. Full of idealism, I looked forward to beginning clinical work with much enthusiasm.

I had two placements, one at the University Counselling Service and the other at the Psychology Department of the Uffculme Clinic, a local psychiatric clinic. I was fortunate in that all my clients were assessed as being able to benefit from person-centred counselling, and thus, I began the practical part of counsellor training under ideal conditions, something that today does not happen as frequently as it should. In my zeal, I did not think about the clients who were not deemed suitable to be counselled by me. I was far too enthusiastic to entertain such questions and doubts. The clients whom I did see were indeed good candidates for person-centred therapy as practised by a trainee, in that they were all reasonably functioning individuals with mild to moderate self-esteem problems.

Initially, I formed good relationships with my clients and they all stated that counselling was helping them to feel better. However, as the counselling proceeded, most of my clients became stuck. They could not get beyond their original gains and began to ask me for advice about how to deal with their problems. I was fleetingly aware that many of them were expressing irrational ideas, since we had considered Rational Emotive Therapy (as it was known then) in our second-term study of other therapeutic approaches. But I was convinced that, if I only persisted in offering empathy, respect and genuineness, my clients would all overcome their 'stuckness' as person-centred theory hypothesized they would. They didn't, however, and I became convinced that the fault lay with me. Of course, I didn't give them any of the advice that they sought – to do so would be to commit one of the cardinal sins of counselling, certainly of the person-centred variety.

Looking back, I think I was partly right in my assessment. My training was strong on helping us to develop the skills of empathy, but I'm not sure that it helped us to develop a truly deep sense of empathy as a way of being, which Rogers (1975) emphasised in an important later paper. In retrospect, I don't think I really engaged any of my clients in a meaningful I–Thou encounter. I think that it was hoped that our participation in the personal development group would help us to do this, but since this was not a person-centred group it was unlikely to help us in this way. Supervision on the course also focused more on the skills of empathic responding than on the other two conditions.

I realise now that, in addition to the above factors, my increasing frustration was really symptomatic of a lack of congruence between me as a person and the practice of person-centred counselling. I still resonated with its theory, but increasingly not with its practice. I should stress that I did not conclude this at the time. No, at the time I alternated between thinking that I was at fault for not being able to offer the requisite core conditions and thinking that the approach was at fault for not offering clients the something extra that many of them were explicitly asking for.

Post diploma training at the Uffculme Clinic, 1975-7

It was while I was in the latter frame of mind, i.e. thinking that the fault lay with person-centred therapy and not with me, that I applied for and was offered a place on the two-year psychodynamic course at the Uffculme Clinic. By this time I had not only qualified as a counsellor from Aston, but had been appointed to the staff! The arrangement that enabled visiting Americans to spend a year at the university as Fulbright fellows had ceased and a full-time position as counsellor trainer had become available. I was encouraged to apply for it (after all, I did hold a Diploma in Counselling *and* a PhD in psychology), and I got the job.

To give the university its due, I had a very gentle introduction to life as an academic. I was mentored by Richard Nelson-Jones and had a very light initial teaching, training and supervision load. This would not happen today, when, if appointed under similar conditions, I would be thrown into the deep end of a full teaching and training timetable.

For the first year at Aston, I led a very split existence. Publicly, I was upholding the virtues of person-centred counselling to the incoming trainees; privately, I was leaving this approach behind as I settled into my psychodynamic course. I should state quite clearly here that this course was not a proper training in psychodynamic therapy as would be understood today; but it was the first training endeavour to be introduced in the Midlands, and beggars can't be choosers. The course, which was held every Tuesday afternoon for two years, was divided in two. The first part of the afternoon was devoted to theory and (later in the course) practice, and the second part to participation in a group, the exact nature of which was not specified. There was no skills training and no supervision.

In my naivety, I had thought that I could begin to practise psychodynamically fairly soon after the course started, but I quickly concluded that I had neither the knowledge nor the temperament for this kind of work. I found the neutral stance of the therapist quite difficult and was unsure about how to make interpretations. Also, during my year at Aston and the year under discussion I had been a client (or, more accurately, a patient) with three psychodynamically oriented therapists, and I just didn't get on with the therapy. It is in the nature of this kind of therapy that you are not supposed to come to such conclusions quickly, so I persisted with it until the coming together of my experiences as a trainee and as a client/patient led me to admit finally that this therapy was not for me either as a practitioner or as a client. Physically I gave up being a patient, and mentally I gave up hopes of becoming a psychodynamic therapist. But I didn't leave the course and managed to complete it, thinking that at least it had shown me what not to believe and how not to practise.

The man with the pink and white check suit

When I first learned about what is now known as Rational Emotive Behaviour Therapy (REBT), I was both attracted to it and repelled by it. I was attracted by its ideas, but repelled by an interview I saw in which Ellis counselled Gloria, a woman who had volunteered to be filmed being interviewed in the mid-1960s by Carl Rogers, Fritz Perls and Albert Ellis.

When I saw the 'Gloria' interviews I was steeped in and embracing the idea that counsellors had to be non-intrusive, gentle and kind. And here was this brash American talking ten to the dozen and recommending to Gloria that it was perfectly in order for her to ask her physician out for a date. And yet, something must have taken hold, because after I had abandoned my final attempt as a client in psychodynamic therapy I read *A New Guide to Rational Living* (Ellis and Harper, 1975); I was attracted to their ideas, applied the techniques to myself, and in fairly short order overcame the mild feelings of anxiety and depression that had prompted me to go into therapy in the first place.

Soon after, in early 1977, I attended a one-day workshop in Rational Emotive Therapy that was held at an American airbase in Suffolk and run by an American psychiatrist named Maxie C. Maultsby Jr. a remarkable man (to me at any rate) in that he was wearing a very loud pink and white check suit! What left a more enduring impression on me, however, was that I suddenly realised that I had found what I had been looking for. Maultsby spoke a lot of sense and showed several videotapes demonstrating that REBT could be practised in a way that involved the client in a more slowly paced dialogue than that shown in the Ellis–Gloria film. To be fair to Ellis, the interview with Gloria was carried out under difficult conditions and, as Ellis now freely admits, it was not a good example of the therapy even as it was practised then. Indeed, it lasted only 18 minutes and Ellis experienced self-imposed pressure to cram too much into this short interview.

At the end of the Maultsby workshop, I joined with several people who resolved to bring over an REBT therapist for a more extended training, with the result that later that year I attended a five-day workshop in REBT given by Virginia Anne Church from San Francisco. This experience clinched things for me, and the following year I embarked on a full training in REBT in New York at the then Institute for Rational Emotive Therapy. The rest is history, and I have been an REBT practitioner ever since.

On reflection, I experienced a congruence between my own ideas, temperament and natural problem-solving tendencies and the theory and practice of REBT. With respect to ideas, I agreed with Ellis that cognitive factors are at the core of our psychological problems. Rogers's view is not too dissimilar, but the language that he uses is less precise and I have always valued precision. With respect to temperament, I tend to favour an active–directive approach to life and realise now that I felt constrained by the active but relatively non-directive approach advocated by person-centred therapy and by the relatively inactive and neutral style advocated by psychodynamic therapy. REBT also resonated closely with my own natural problem-solving tendencies. Let me dwell on this particular issue at some length.

In my youth, I had a stammer and made myself quite anxious about speaking in public. I tried a number of speech therapists, who were unable to help me either with my anxiety about my stammer or with the stammer itself. It was only when I heard Michael Bentine explain on the radio how he conquered his stammer-related anxiety that I was given the help that I needed. Bentine helped himself by convincing himself that if he stammered, he stammered – too bad. I embellished this somewhat and convinced myself that if I stammered, I stammered – *fuck it*! Using this philosophy, I resolved to speak in public at every possibility, as opposed to my usual pattern of ducking out of speaking in public whenever I could. After a while, I found to my great satisfaction that I lost my anxiety about speaking in public. I still stammered from time to time, although far less so than hitherto, but anxious I was not. Since that time I have spoken and stammered on radio, television and in large public lectures that I have delivered, and undeterred, I press on. Disfluency rules OK!

As I examine it now, what I did then was very much in keeping with REBT theory and practice. I practised a healthy philosophy both cognitively and behaviourally. I really convinced myself of my new philosophy by using a forceful self-statement, and I persisted with this form of self-help until I had eradicated my anxiety. Also, I avoided my tendency to avoid, and thus prevented myself from relapsing. I hadn't then heard about counselling, let alone REBT, yet there I was practising REBT on myself. Remember too that years later I helped myself to get over my mild anxiety and depression by reading an REBT self-help book and applying what I had read.

Conclusion

I no longer practise person-centred therapy (PCT) or psychodynamic therapy because I disagree with person-centred practice and with both the theory and practice of psychodynamic therapy. My ideas about how humans disturb themselves and what can be done to help them, and to help them help themselves, resonate very closely with the theory and practice of REBT. I like and agree with its emphasis on psychological education, and I experience a sense of congruence between my penchant for being active–directive in my personal life and the emphasis that REBT places on the therapist being active and directive in his professional life. I experience a sense of genuineness when I practise REBT that I never experienced when practising PCT and (fleetingly) psychodynamic therapy, because I have used its ideas to help myself and I continue to do so.

Do I then conclude that REBT is necessarily a better or more effective therapy than the two other approaches that I used to practise but later gave up? Not at all. Do I say that all clients will benefit from REBT? No. Clients have their own ideas about what will be helpful to them and what will not. Some do and others do not resonate with the active–directive and psychoeducational nature of REBT, for instance. However, since REBT therapists believe in being explicit about the therapy, clients are likely to discover this sooner rather than later and to save themselves valuable time and money. Finally, am I urging you to abandon your studies and come to train in REBT with me? You can if you like, but this is not my intention.

My intention has been to help you to reflect, through hearing about my own personal and professional journey, on the degree of congruence between yourself as a person, and in particular your ideas, temperament and natural problem-solving tendencies, and the therapy that you practise. If you experience such congruence, fine, but if not maybe it is time to embark on a similar journey that I took twenty years ago.

Of course, there are other important factors to being a counsellor than the congruence between yourself and the approach you practise. But without such congruence, will you truly embrace the tenets of this approach and thus be an effective practitioner? Here I can only answer for myself. I could never become an effective person-centred or psychodynamic practitioner because I could not personally resonate with the central tenets of these approaches. This realisation was painful, but ultimately fruitful.

References

Ellis, A., & Harper, R. (1975). *A new guide to rational living.* North: Hollywood, CA: Wilshire.

Jourard, S.M. (1971). *The transparent self.* New York: Van Nostrand Reinhold.

Rogers, C.R. (1957). The necessary and sufficient conditions of therapeutic personality change. *Journal of Consulting Psychology,* 21, 95-103.

Rogers, C.R. (1975). Empathic: an unappreciated way of being. The *Counseling Psychologist*, 5 (2), 2-10.

4

rational emotive behaviour therapy: why I practise an approach to counselling that is unpopular

This lecture develops the theme that I first took up in the previous chapter and was delivered to the Wessex affiliated branch of the British Association for Counselling at Bournemouth on June 18, 1997. At the end of the lecture I went to dinner with a small group which included my friend and colleague, Albert Kushlik who had driven over from Southampton to hear my lecture. He was on top form and enjoyed the dinner tremendously. Sadly, it was the last time I saw Albert alive for he died later that year. I dedicate this book to his memory.

Which approach do most counsellors in Britain practise? My guess is that it is either psychodynamic counselling or person-centred counselling. One thing is clear: it is not Rational Emotive Behaviour Therapy. In this lecture I will make clear why I practise an approach to counselling that is not only manifestly *not* popular, but is also in all probability *un*popular.

Let me state at the outset that I am not unduly troubled about this state of affairs. Indeed, it probably suits me psychologically, for I have never been very comfortable being involved with anything that is popular. I am something of a loner, and practising an approach to counselling that has many practitioners would not appeal to me. However, this does not fully explain why I practise REBT, since if I really wanted to be on my own in Britain I would practise Reality Therapy or Morita Therapy, both of which have very few advocates in this country. No, aside from this psychological fit, I practise REBT for reasons that have much more to do with its theoretical principles and its stance on practice. In this lecture I will discuss these factors and point to ways in which they contrast with more popular thinking about counselling theory and practice.

First, let me explain why I think REBT is unpopular rather than merely not popular. The roots of this unpopularity can be traced back to the 'Gloria' film, in which a client known as Gloria (now sadly deceased) was counselled by three famous therapists: Carl Rogers, Fritz Perls and Albert Ellis. This film was made in the mid-1960s, and for many years it was routinely shown to trainees on counselling courses up and down the country – for all I know it is still shown in some quarters. Ellis's interview with Gloria is the third of the screened interviews and lasts approximately 18 minutes. With Ellis, Gloria spoke mainly about her difficulties in meeting eligible men and Ellis seemed to suggest that it was perfectly acceptable for her to ask her physician out for a date, a practice that at the very least is frowned on today and is more likely to be viewed as encouraging the client to invite her GP to act unethically. Ellis has admitted that it was not a good example of REBT even as it was practised then. He tried to cram too much into the interview, with the result that Gloria seems confused at various points in the session. The point that I would like to make to you is this: would you be happy to be judged on your current work by work that you did for 18 minutes over thirty years ago and in difficult circumstances?

Another reason why REBT is unpopular in Britain is due to what people have heard about Ellis's personality and behaviour. Stories have circulated that he is rude, unsociable, bad-tempered, freely uses profanity in his workshops and with clients, and is openly contemptuous of other approaches to counselling and psychotherapy. Like many rumours, there is a grain of truth to these criticisms, but they have been blown out of proportion. Indeed, many people have found Ellis to be exceptionally kind and encouraging, and in a small-scale survey of some of his clients conducted by my colleague Joseph Yankura and myself, they said that they regarded Ellis as remarkably accepting of them and that they felt they could tell him anything and he would not be shocked (Yankura & Dryden, 1990). This side of Ellis rarely sees the light of day.

In any case, it is unfair to criticise a therapy system such as REBT because of the behaviour of one its practitioners, even if that practitioner is the founder of the therapy. Let me state unequivocally that you do not have to model yourself after Albert Ellis to be an effective Rational Emotive Behaviour Therapist. And let me repeat that Ellis's behaviour as a therapist is not nearly as outrageous as some people have made out.

REBT is also unpopular for reasons unconnected with the behaviour or personality of Albert Ellis. Thus, it is unpopular because it is a directive and structured approach to counselling. This is the antithesis of the psychodynamic and person-centred approaches. While there is no such thing as a non-directive approach to therapy, in that, even if you remain totally silent during a counselling session, doing so represents taking a direction in the interview, it is true to say that counselling approaches vary from being highly directive to being less directive. I practise REBT because it is directive. As I will presently show, REBT – like other approaches to counselling – has a perspective on psychological disturbance, and REBT counsellors direct their clients to this perspective in an explicit way so that the latter can decide whether or not this perspective will be of benefit to them. In other words, REBT counsellors elicit their clients' informed consent about participating in this therapy approach; once this consent is given, they direct their clients to the REBT model of psychological disturbance so that the clients can begin to help themselves in a time-efficient manner. I should add that effective REBT therapists are sensitive to their clients' readiness for such a directive approach and will be less directive when the situation calls for it. Believe it or not, good REBT therapists are sensitive and flexible practitioners.

I mentioned that REBT is, by and large, a structured approach to counselling. As such, it is often criticised for not giving clients an opportunity to explore themselves in an unstructured manner. This criticism is understandable, but incorrect. It is understandable because whenever REBT therapists give demonstrations of REBT we are keen to show its distinctive features, and thus we tend to emphasise REBT's structured and directive approach. However, in actual practice there is nothing in REBT theory and practice that forbids its practitioners from giving clients an unfettered opportunity to explore themselves in their own way at various times in the counselling process, although structure informed by REBT principles will be brought to REBT counselling sooner or later – otherwise the work will become unfocused and unproductive. In my experience as a counselling trainer and supervisor and as an external examiner, I have heard many tapes in which it was clear that the client was becoming thoroughly confused precisely because the counsellor failed to provide sufficient structure to the interview, structure that would have helped the client to use counselling much more productively.

I have discussed elsewhere the personal underpinnings of my choice of REBT as a counselling orientation (see Chapter 3 above). Briefly, it suits my temperament, and there is a close relationship between my natural problem-solving tendencies and the approach to emotional problem-solving advocated by REBT. What I will emphasise here concerns selected elements of the theory and practice of REBT that I consider particularly therapeutic.

The empowering aspects of the ABC framework

REBT has, from its inception, advocated an ABC theory of psychological disturbance, where A stands for an Activating event, B for the person's Beliefs about this event, and C for the emotional, behavioural and cognitive Consequences of holding these beliefs. This model is very empowering for clients in that it shows them that they are not passive reactors to life events and that, while they will inevitably be influenced by these events, they have the power not to disturb themselves about them, (Anne Walker, personal communication, 1996.)

While other counselling approaches take a similar phenomenological line, REBT is unique in being very precise about the beliefs that are at the core of psychological disturbance and those that are at the core of psychological health. It is this precision that I find particularly useful in that it helps clients to identify their own unhealthy beliefs when they feel emotionally disturbed. For those of you who are unfamiliar with REBT's theory, it posits four major unhealthy beliefs (demandingness, awfulising, low frustration tolerance, and deprecation of self, others and/or life conditions) and four major healthy beliefs (preferences, anti-awfulising, high frustration tolerance and acceptance of self, others and/or life conditions). It follows that a major goal for REBT counsellors is to encourage clients to surrender their unhealthy beliefs and to develop their healthy beliefs.

REBT counsellors have been heavily criticised for forcing the ABC model on to their clients and for preventing the development of their clients' inherent tendencies to actualise themselves. Both of these criticisms are unwarranted in my view. REBT counsellors do offer their clients a particular perspective on psychological problems and their remediation. But, as I said earlier, in keeping with good ethical practice, we spell out this framework and its implications for client participation early in the counselling process to enable clients to make an informed decision about whether or not they wish to commit themselves to this form of counselling. As such, effective REBT therapists abide by the principle of informed consent and certainly do not impose the ABC framework on their clients.

In response to the criticism that, by offering a particular framework for understanding personal problems and their remediation, REBT counsellors interfere with their clients' self-actualising tendencies, I would argue as follows. REBT recognises that humans have a drive towards self-actualisation, but it also states that we have a strong tendency to disturb ourselves and to easily prevent ourselves from remaining on this arduous, life-long path. REBT counsellors view the ABC framework for understanding personal problems as a tool to help clients stay on this path. They differ from their humanistic colleagues in their view that, in taking the road towards self-actualisation, clients often need a map to understand the obstacles they will encounter along the way and a variety of tools or techniques to help them surmount these obstacles. In this way, REBT promotes rather than inhibits the process of self-actualisation.

The distinction between healthy and unhealthy negative emotions
As far as I am aware, REBT is the only therapeutic approach that keenly differentiates between healthy and unhealthy negative emotions. Yes, I did say *healthy* negative emotions. When a client is confronted by a negative activating event at A, it is healthy for her (in this case) to feel badly about this event. We don't want the client to have good feelings about a negative event, nor do we want her to feel indifferent about it. However, in stating that it is healthy for clients to feel bad about bad events, REBT recognises that it is easy for clients to have disturbed negative feelings rather than healthy negative feelings about negative activating events. How are we to differentiate between the two? REBT theory argues that healthy and unhealthy negative emotions can be distinguished as follows:

i. Unhealthy negative emotions (such as anxiety; depression; guilt; hurt; shame; demanding, condemnatory anger; unhealthy envy and jealousy) stem from irrational beliefs, while healthy negative emotions (such as concern; sadness; remorse; sorrow; disappointment; non-demanding, non-blaming anger; healthy envy and concern for one's relationship) stem from rational beliefs.

ii. Unhealthy negative emotions are associated with actions and action tendencies that are self-defeating and relationship-defeating and impede the pursuit of one's personally meaningful goals, whereas healthy negative emotions are associated with actions and action tendencies that are self-enhancing and relationship-enhancing and that facilitate the pursuit of one's personally meaningful goals.

iii. Unhealthy negative emotions (and the irrational beliefs that underpin them) lead to distorted, negative inferences (Bond & Dryden, 1996) and blinkered attention, while healthy negative emotions lead to reality-based inferences (Bond & Dryden, 1996) and non-blinkered attention.

A major goal of REBT is to help clients experience healthy negative emotions rather than unhealthy negative emotions about negative activating events. It is important to realise that healthy negative emotions can be of equal intensity to their unhealthy counterparts. Thus, REBT counsellors do not endeavour to help clients reduce the intensity of unhealthy negative emotions since less unhealthy negative emotions, are still regarded as unhealthy. Experiencing healthy negative emotions of whatever intensity enables clients to adjust constructively to negative activating events and move on, while unhealthy negative emotions lead to clients becoming bogged down and stuck, unable to adjust constructively to these negative events and unable to move on. Healthy negative emotions thus promote coping and learning from experience, while unhealthy negative emotions interfere with coping and inhibit learning from experience.

REBT's position on self-acceptance
REBT has a unique position on self-esteem which avoids many of the difficulties associated with this concept. Basically, REBT theory considers the concept of self-esteem to be pernicious and discourages clients from improving their self-esteem. Instead, REBT counsellors encourage their clients to work towards unconditional self-acceptance.

Let's have a close look at the concept of self-esteem and then consider why REBT is against this concept. In REBT, the 'self' is defined as 'every conceivable thing about you that can be rated' (Hauck, 1991) and 'esteem' is derived from the verb 'to estimate', which means to rate or to judge something. REBT's position is that it is impossible legitimately to give the 'self' a single global rating because the self is far too complex to merit such a rating. It is also constantly in flux, so that, even if it could be legitimately rated, it would have changed as soon as the rating was made. In addition, as soon as you ask people to tell you what would improve their self-esteem, it becomes clear that, even if they were to achieve high self-esteem, it would be a tenuous state. Thus, if someone says that being loved would improve his (in this case) self-esteem, that person would also acknowledge that his self-esteem would plummet if the other person were to cease to love him.

Unconditional self-acceptance is a better alternative to self-esteem for several reasons. First, it involves the person acknowledging that he is a unique, fallible human being who is constantly changing and is too complex to merit a single global rating.

Second, unconditional self-acceptance does not preclude the person from taking responsibility for aspects of himself. When a person takes responsibility for that which is within his purview without rating himself, he is more likely to work constructively towards changing aspects of himself that he does not like than would be the case if such responsibility were underpinned by self-rating. If you rate your 'self' negatively for aspects of yourself that you do not like, you tend to focus on your negative self-rating rather than working towards changing those negatively rated aspects.

Third, if the person accepts himself unconditionally, he is not anxious about losing love, for example, because he does not base his worth on being loved. This does not mean that the person will be indifferent towards losing love. Unconditional self-acceptance encourages the person to be concerned (but not anxious) about the loss of love, and this is regarded as a healthy response to the prospect of losing something that is important to the person.

Finally, unconditional self-acceptance helps the person to accept other people unconditionally as unique, fallible human beings with good, bad and neutral aspects, and thus facilitates good egalitarian relationships with others. In contrast, self-esteem leads to problematic relationships with others. Thus, when a person rates himself negatively, he will either tend to rate others negatively – a situation that leads to increased conflict in relationships – or to rate others too positively – a situation that leads to dependency and naivety.

REBT's focus on discomfort disturbance
REBT distinguishes clearly between *ego disturbance* and *discomfort disturbance*. In ego disturbance, a person holds a belief about herself (in this case) that is self-deprecating in nature (e.g. I am a failure), whereas in discomfort disturbance the person believes that she cannot tolerate something that it is in her interest to tolerate. While ego disturbance and discomfort disturbance frequently co-exist in people's problems (e.g. in addictions) and frequently interact with each other, it is important to work on them separately if as a counsellor you are to avoid becoming hopelessly lost when dealing with complex client problems. REBT theory helps me to understand these two different

types of psychological disturbance and to respond with different interventions suited to each.

REBT's focus on meta-emotional problems

REBT theory hypothesises that clients often (although not always) have meta-emotional problems. A meta-emotional problem can be defined as an emotional problem about an emotional problem. Thus, if a client is depressed about the loss of his job (in this case) and is ashamed about being depressed, his depression can be seen as his original emotional problem and his shame about his depression as his meta-emotional problem.

The REBT view of counselling practice specifies when it may be particularly important to help clients deal with their meta-emotional problems before dealing with their original emotional problems. Thus, I recommend working on a meta-emotional problem first (i) when this problem is clinically the most important of the two (as in generalised anxiety disorder, for example); (ii) when the existence of this problem will interfere with the work you will do with your client's original problem in the counselling session (e.g. if the client becomes preoccupied with feelings of shame as you focus on his depression); and (iii) when the existence of the meta-emotional problem interferes with the work that the client needs to do on his original problem between counselling sessions (e.g. when the client makes himself anxious (meta-emotional problem) about his anxiety about speaking in public (original emotional problem)).

Thus, I find that the concept of meta-emotional problems is particularly useful when understanding a person in the context of his problems and when planning counselling strategies over time.

REBT's view of therapeutic change

REBT has a definite view of therapeutic change which, while unattractive to many clients, is realistic and can help sustain clients when the going gets tough for them. This view stresses that changing irrational beliefs is at the heart of long-term therapeutic change. While clients can benefit in the shorter term by changing their inferences (or interpretations) about negative activating events, by modifying their behaviour when faced with these events or by removing themselves from the events, such strategies do not tend to help them deal effectively with these and similar negative activating events in the future. Thus, facilitating belief change is the objective of REBT therapists.

Clients begin the process of changing irrational beliefs to their rational counterparts by first understanding why their irrational beliefs are irrational and why their alternative rational beliefs are rational. This is so-called *intellectual insight* and is an important first step in the belief change process. However, on its own, such intellectual insight will not promote long-term therapeutic change because the person has not integrated her (in this case) rational beliefs into her belief system. Such integration means that the new rational beliefs have a significant impact on how the client feels, acts and thinks. This integration is brought about by the client repeatedly acting in ways that are consistent with the new rational beliefs and by refusing to act in ways that are consistent with the older irrational beliefs.

In order to sustain this process of weakening conviction in one's irrational beliefs and strengthening conviction in one's rational beliefs, the client needs to keep in mind four points. First, she needs to have a clear idea that changing her beliefs in this way will lead her to achieve her desired therapeutic goals. Second, she needs to realise that the process of change is difficult and uncomfortable and that it would be easy to gain immediate comfort by going back to familiar patterns of behaviour which although self-defeating are comfortable because of their familiarity. Third, she needs to embrace the idea that therapeutic change is rarely linear and that she will, in all probability, experience setbacks along the way. If she refuses to be disturbed by these setbacks, she can learn from them and get back on the path towards personal change. The fourth and final point that the client would be wise to acknowledge is that, even when she has made a great deal of progress and has consistently acted in a way that is in keeping with her increasingly believed rational ideas, it will still be very easy for her to slip back into old unhealthy patterns of thinking and behaving; consequently, some form of life-long commitment to personal development work and associated vigilance will be necessary.

As you can probably imagine, many clients are not exactly thrilled by this 'Protestant ethic' perspective on therapeutic change, but it is valuable to them in the long term because in my view it is realistic and reflects the difficulties that we all have as human beings in sustaining meaningful personal change. Here as elsewhere, we REBT therapists do not take an overly consumeristic line and tell the punters what they want to hear (Ellis, 1989): rather, we tell it like we believe it is, even if it is somewhat unpalatable. In some respects, REBT is the cod liver oil of the counselling world!

REBT's position on the value of the therapeutic alliance
Like virtually all approaches to counselling and psychotherapy, REBT regards the development and maintenance of a good working alliance between the counsellor and client as a very important therapeutic ingredient (Bordin, 1979). Thus, it holds that it is important that the counsellor and client agree on the goals of counselling, and it stresses that each participant needs to understand and agree to the tasks that

both are called upon to carry out in the pursuit of these goals. Finally, it holds that a good bond between counsellor and client facilitates the counselling process.

However, REBT does not hold that the therapeutic relationship is the sine qua non of counselling. Its position on the 'core conditions' issue is virtually unchanged from Ellis's (1959) original view, which he outlined in a response to Rogers's (1957) seminal article on this topic. This position holds that, while it is important for the client to experience the counsellor as empathic, respectful and genuine in the therapeutic encounter, these conditions are neither necessary nor sufficient for therapeutic change to occur. This makes the REBT approach unpopular with person-centred counsellors, who do hold that these conditions are necessary and sufficient for change to occur.

Furthermore, REBT counsellors strive to develop and maintain an adult-to-adult relationship with clients. Clients are treated as adults who have views about what will benefit them and who need to understand the nature of REBT before they can be expected to give their informed consent for receiving this form of counselling. This means that, at the outset and throughout the counselling process, REBT counsellors will be explicit about their therapeutic intentions and activities and will elicit their clients' agreement to play their part in the process as adult consumers who need to be informed throughout the counselling if they are to participate fully in the process.

REBT counsellors do not think that it is important to look for and interpret clients' transferential reactions. This not to say that we do not recognise that such reactions exist. It is just that we do not go out of our way to encourage them. When they do emerge, we tend to help clients to look for, examine, challenge and change the irrational beliefs that underpin these transferential reactions. As you can tell, this puts REBT therapists at variance with our psychodynamic colleagues, who tend to view transference and its resolution as a more central part of the therapeutic process. Also, our psychodynamic colleagues tend not to be as explicit about therapy as we are.

REBT's psycho-educational approach

I have practised REBT for twenty years and now see it as a psycho-educational approach to counselling. I see effective REBT therapists as practitioners who:

    i.   are explicit about the way REBT theory conceptualises clients' difficulties;

    ii. explain both their role as REBT counsellors and their clients' role as REBT clients;

iii. elicit their clients' informed consent to proceed in counselling;

iv. teach clients the REBT skills of assessment and intervention so that they can learn to become their own therapists; and

v. outline the REBT view of therapeutic change so that clients can have a realistic view of what they have to do to initiate and sustain personal change. In particular, this involves clients making a commitment to undertake a range of homework assignments which are designed to help them to change their irrational beliefs and to deepen their conviction in their new rational beliefs.

In performing these tasks, effective REBT therapists wherever possible adopt an active–directive style, particularly at the beginning of the counselling process after they have given their clients an opportunity to explore themselves in their own way. As I mentioned earlier, this is perhaps one of the aspects of REBT that make it so unpopular with the majority of counsellors in Britain. However, as counselling proceeds, REBT therapists become less active and less directive, particularly as clients begin to take increasing responsibility for facilitating their own change.

In conclusion, I have never bothered too much that REBT is unpopular in Britain. Although I have an interest in seeing REBT develop, I do not think that it is right for me to present it in ways that make it attractive to counsellors but disguise its intrinsic nature. In true REBT fashion, I think it would be nice if you all wanted to become REBT therapists on the basis of my presentation; however if none of you did, that would be sad, but hardly the end of the world.

References

Bond, F.W., & Dryden, W. (1996). Modifying irrational control and certainty beliefs: clinical recommendations based upon research. In W. Dryden (ed.), *Research in counselling and psychotherapy*. London: Sage.

Bordin, E.S. (1979). The generalizability of the psychoanalytic concept of the working alliance. *Psychotherapy: Theory, Research and Practice*, 16, 252-260.

Dryden, W. (1997). *Why I no longer practise person-centred therapy and psychodynamic therapy : some personal reflections*. Lecture given to the MSc Counselling Psychology course, University of East London, 25 April; reprinted as Chapter 3 above.

Ellis, A. (1959). Requisite conditions for basic personality change. *Journal of Consulting Psychology*, 23, 538-540.

Ellis, A. (1989). Ineffective consumerism in the cognitive-behavioural therapies and in general psychotherapy. In W. Dryden & P. Trower (eds.), *Cognitive psychotherapy: stasis and change.* London: Cassell.

Hauck, P. (1991). *Hold your head up high.* London: Sheldon.

Rogers, C.R. (1957). The necessary and sufficient conditions of therapeutic personality change. *Journal of Consulting Psychology*, 21, 95-103.

Yankura, J., & Dryden, W. (1990). *Doing RET: Albert Ellis in action.* New York: Springer.

5

the counsellor as educator: promise, possibilities and problems

This paper was delivered as the Frank Lake Memorial Lecture at Bourneville College, Birmingham on July 11, 1996. This annual series of lectures was established by the Clinical Theology Association (CTA) for the purpose of inviting appropriate people to reflect on their own work and at the same time help develop an possibly indicate new directions for the Association's objectives.

I had given a previous version of the lecture at the European Association for Counselling conference in Dublin where it was viewed as controversial and led to one member of the audience loudly walking out during question time. I still do not regard this lecture as controversial, but it does challenge traditional views of counselling.

The lecture was published by the CTA as the 24th Lingdale Paper and is currently in print and available from the Association at St Mary's House, Church Westcote, Oxford, OX7 6SF.

One can think of a counsellor as an educator, and a client as a learner. This educator–learner simile for the counsellor–client relationship is, of course, only one of a number that exist in the counselling and psychotherapy literature. Don Bannister discussed five such similes: doctor–patient, trainer–trainee, friend–friend, priest–penitent and supervisor–researcher (Bannister, 1983). Perhaps facilitator–developer – one of the most popular similes for this relationship – is at the heart of humanistic approaches to counselling, which together with psychodynamic approaches dominate the counselling scene in Britain.

In considering the counsellor as an educator, I shall refer to my experiences both as a counsellor and as a client. Although these experiences should not be considered prescriptions for how all counselling should be practised, some of my experiences as a client may well be shared by others.

Psychological education

One of the most profound statements I have come across in the counselling and psychotherapy literature was made by an American psychiatrist, Maxie C. Maultsby Jr: 'No method of counselling works unless the person being counselled decides to use it' (Maultsby, 1975). If this is true, and I prejudicially think it is, then it implies that effective counselling is ultimately effective self-counselling. There are two ways to approach the issue of self-counselling: one can approach it systematically or one can leave it to chance. Most counselling leaves to chance what clients learn and take away from the process.

If the counsellor is an educator, she is a specific kind of educator. She educates in the area that spans human thought and imagery, emotions, behaviour, sensations and relationships. Broadly speaking, this area is known as psychology. So, more specifically, the counsellor can be seen as a psycho-educator, and I will refer to the terms 'educator' and 'psycho-educator' synonymously.

The idea that a counsellor is a psychological educator has not gained much support from the field, although several people have written about it. Richard Nelson-Jones, previously a colleague of mine at the University of Aston in Birmingham, noted that there are six broad uses of the term 'psychological education'. It encompasses:
 i. training people in life skills;
 ii. combining academic and experiential approaches to the teaching of psychology;
 iii. humanistic education;
 iv. training paraprofessionals in counselling skills;
 v. running a range of counselling outreach activities;
 vi. educating the general public in psychological matters. (Nelson-Jones, 1982).

I shall touch on several of these issues, but will focus on the application of one particular counselling approach – Rational Emotive Behaviour Therapy (REBT) (Dryden,1995) – in a way that attempts to 'give it away' to clients so that they can learn to use its framework and skills to help themselves. Although I practise REBT, what I have to say is, I believe, applicable to other approaches too.

In this context, I define psycho-education as the systematic approach to helping clients use the method of counselling advocated by the counsellor. Many would object to this view because it directly challenges their own view of the nature of the counsellor–client relationship. Am I advocating that counsellors explicitly teach their clients counselling methods? That we should in effect 'give counselling away' to our clients? Well, yes and no. I do not wish to persuade counsellors to practise as I do – only to consider the merits of another way of construing counselling and one that may benefit some of their clients.

I have been in this profession too long to ignore a basic fact which psychology students are taught on their first day: that clients are different from one another. Not all of them will benefit from one particular kind of therapy. If there are counsellors who claim otherwise, my advice is to avoid them, at least professionally. What follows from this is that we need to match client to therapy, and if what I have to offer does not suit the client in front of me, I should 'refer in'. (I do this routinely, although the issues that this viewpoint raises are outside the scope of this lecture.)

However, even when a client is matched with an approach to counselling that is best suited to his problems and the way that he conceptualizes them, Maultsby's basic point still holds: that counselling will work to the extent that the client uses the methods that he learns explicitly or implicitly from the counselling endeavour.

Educating clients in their tasks

I defined psycho-education as 'the systematic approach to helping clients use the method of counselling advocated by the counsellor'. People may object to this statement for another reason. It may seem that the counsellor has in mind what clients need to do in counselling sessions and in their everyday lives, and that this is far too prescriptive. But do not all counselling approaches have explicit or, more frequently, implicit tasks with which clients have to engage? I believe they do. Are not clients of psychodynamic therapists called upon to engage in 'free associative processes' and clients of humanistic counsellors to engage in the tasks of self-exploration? I agree that these tasks are broad in nature, but they are tasks none the less. In REBT they are as follows:

The client's tasks

1. Specify problems.
2. Be open to the therapist's REBT framework.
3. Apply the specific principle of emotional responsibility, that people disturb themselves by holding sets of irrational beliefs about actual or inferred negative events.
4. Apply the principle of therapeutic responsibility, that in order to achieve therapeutic change the client needs to put into practice in his everyday life the change tactics that he learns in therapy sessions.
5. Disclose doubts about REBT concepts, difficulties in applying these concepts and other obstacles to personal change.

The psycho-educational approach to counselling states that it is important for REBT counsellors to deliberately train clients to engage effectively in these tasks, rather than to leave this to chance. My hypothesis is that counsellors from other orientations would also help their clients more if they explicitly trained them to engage in the tasks that the orientation asks them to carry out. There is research that confirms this hypothesis. One of the most robust findings to emerge from psychotherapy research shows that, when clients are educated in their role and the tasks that are associated with this role before they see their therapists, they then achieve more positive outcomes than clients who do not receive such pre-therapy training. (Garfield, 1994).

Gaining informed consent from clients
The psycho-educational approach to counselling is based on the idea that counsellors need to be explicit about their role in the counselling process and that of their clients. As such, it is very much in accord with the principle of informed consent. Many professional codes of ethics and practice in counselling and psychotherapy advocate that clients give their informed consent before therapeutic techniques can be ethically used with them. This consent can be given only when clients understand both their counsellors' tasks and their own.

I have just outlined what the client's five tasks are in REBT. I make these tasks explicit at the outset of counselling precisely because it helps my client to make an informed decision about whether or not REBT is likely to be of use to her. In doing so, I explain these tasks in a way that she is likely to understand, omitting any REBT jargon. Thus, I may say something like this:

> *'All approaches to counselling require something from clients if*
> *counselling is to be effective. In the approach that I practise, I'll ask*
> *you to specify your problems as clearly as you can. Then I'll offer you*
> *a framework which I hope will help you to understand what has led to*
> *the development and maintenance of your problems. Your task here is*
> *to listen to my explanation with an open mind. If this framework makes*
> *sense to you, I'll help you to apply it to your problems and suggest*
> *ways in which you can tackle these problems in your everyday life. If*
> *you agree to act on these suggestions, then it's your responsibility to*
> *put these into practice in your daily life. Your last task is to be as*
> *honest as possible about any doubts you have about the framework I*
> *put to you, about any difficulties you have putting into practice what*
> *you learn from me and about any other obstacles that may interfere*
> *with counselling. During the counselling I'll help you to perform these*
> *tasks so that you'll get the most from counselling.'*

If I present the above material without a break, as I have just done, I
then invite my client to give her reaction to what I have said and answer
any questions she may have about her tasks. Usually, however, I would
pause at various points, discuss salient issues and respond to queries
before proceeding to the next point. If what I have said makes sense to
the client, I ask her to give her informed consent to proceed. If, instead,
she indicates that she is looking for a different kind of therapy, I will
gladly offer to refer her to a therapist who practises an approach
consistent with her expectations.

If the client wishes to proceed, this is not the end of the education
process. Far from it. At every stage, I outline explicitly what is required
of the client and will negotiate with her any modification to her tasks.
As counselling proceeds and she becomes more familiar with REBT
concepts, my explanations will reflect her increasing knowledge and
probably will include more REBT jargon.

Explaining a counsellor's role and associated tasks to clients
I outline my tasks to clients at the outset of therapy, so that they may
decide in an informed way whether or not to proceed with REBT; the
box (see page 65) shows how they change during the therapeutic process.
Thus, I might say something like:

> *'I see my role in counselling in the following terms. First I'll listen*
> *to and try to understand your problems and help you to work out*
> *what you want to achieve from counselling. Then I'll explain to you*
> *something about the therapy that I practise. Since I believe that the*
> *best way forward is to deal with your problems*

The counsellor's tasks

The beginning stage
1. Establish a therapeutic alliance by encouraging the client to outline her problems, responding empathically and helping her to set therapeutic goals.
2. Socialize the client into REBT.
3. Begin to assess and intervene in the client's target problem.
4. Teach the ABCDE of REBT, where A stands for an actual or inferred activating event, B for the client's beliefs about this event, C for the emotional and behavioural consequences of these beliefs, D for disputing those of the client's belief that are self-defeating or irrational, and E for the effects of these disputing strategies.
5. Identify and deal with the client's doubts.

The middle stage
6. Persevere with the client's target problem.
7. Encourage the client to engage in relevant change-related tasks both inside therapy sessions and in her everyday life.
8. Work on the client's other problems.
9. Identify and encourage the client to change her underlying irrational beliefs.
10. Identify and deal with her obstacles to change.
11. Encourage her to maintain and enhance her gains.
12. Help her to prevent any relapse, and deal with vulnerability factors.
13. Encourage her to become her own counsellor.

The end stage
14. Decide with the client how and when to end the counselling.
15. Encourage her to summarize what she has learned.
16. Show her what her efforts have achieved.
17. Deal with obstacles to ending the counselling.
18. Agree with her about the criteria for follow-ups and resuming therapy.

---

one at a time, we'll begin to work on the problem you want to start with. In doing so I'll outline a framework for understanding this problem and particularly help you to identify the beliefs that are at its core. Here and elsewhere, I'll encourage you to ask questions about my view of your problem and to voice any doubts you may have about my approach.

Then I'll suggest various techniques that you can use inside and outside the therapy sessions to confront the beliefs that I think are at the core of your first problem. After we have made some progress with your first problem, we'll begin to deal with others. As we do so, I'll be looking to identify a few fundamental irrational beliefs that might account for all your problems. When we find them, I'll suggest how you might change them. As you begin to make progress with your problems, I'll suggest how you might maintain and continue with this progress and how you might prevent any relapse. Then I'll show you how you might become your own counsellor, so that you can deal on your own with any future problems that might develop. At this point, we'll discuss how we might end the therapy and we'll review what you have learned. Finally, we'll make arrangements for any follow-up sessions and discuss the conditions under which you might resume therapy if you need to in the future.'

Although I have presented the tasks as a fairly lengthy monologue, in practice I would regularly pause to gauge my client's reaction to what I have said, to discuss any issues that she wishes to raise and to answer any questions she might have. Then, just as I would have done after outlining her own tasks, I would ask the client if she wishes to proceed. Whether she does or requires a different way of tackling her problems, her decision will be an informed one. If the latter is the case, I would again be happy to effect a suitable referral.

Training clients to carry out their tasks
It is important to spell out for clients the task that they and their counsellors will be called upon to carry out in REBT; but perhaps the heart of the psycho-educational approach to counselling lies in training clients to *execute* their tasks effectively. Although pre-therapy training is important, I shall focus here on the training that clients are given once therapy has begun. In dealing with this issue, I shall again draw upon my work as an REBT therapist. Some clients are able to put REBT assessment methods and therapeutic techniques into practice without being taught specifically how to do so. However, such clients are few, and my hypothesis is that for REBT to have its greatest impact clients need to be deliberately trained to use its assessment methods and therapeutic techniques.

The box shows one example of how I train my clients to assess and deal with their own problems, using the ABCDE framework that I described earlier. It is a version of a form I ask them to fill in, together with some explanatory notes to help them complete the form.

ABC of emotional and behavioural problems

A

C

Major unhealthy negative emotion:

Major self-defeating behaviour:

A = Activating event
- Describe the aspect of the situation you were most disturbed about.
- Assume temporarily that A is true.
- An A can be internal or external.
- An A can refer to an event in the past, present or future.
- An A can be an inference

C = Consequence
Unhealthy negative emotions
- anxiety
- depression
- guilt
- shame and embarrassment
- hurt
- jealousy

iB

D

Dogmatic demand:	Is it true? Is it logical? Is it helpful?
Awfulizing:	Is it true? Is it logical? Is it helpful?
Low frustration tolerance:	Is it true? Is it logical? Is it helpful?
Self/other downing:	Is it true? Is it logical? Is it helpful?

iB = Irrational belief
Look for:
- dogmatic demands (musts, absolute should, oughts)
- awfulizing (it's awful, terrible, horrible)
- low frustration tolerance (I can't stand it, I can't bear it)
- self/other downing (bad, wothless, less worthy)

D = Disputing
- Where is the evidence to support your irrational belief? Is it consistent with reality?
- Is your belief logical? Does it logically follow from your rational belief?
- Where is holding this belief getting you? Is it helpful?

rB	E
Non-dogmatic preference:	New healthy negative emotion:
Evaluating badness:	
High-frustration tolerance:	New constructive behaviour:
Self/other acceptance:	

rB = Rational belief
Strive for:
• non-dogmatic preferences
  (wishes, wants desires)
• evaluating badness
  (it's bad, unfortunate)
• high-frustration tolerance
  (I can stand it, I can bear it)
• self/other acceptance
  ('fallible human being'
  concept)

D = Disputing
Healthy negative emotions:
• concern
• sadness
• annoyance
• remorse
• disappointment
• regret
• concern about your
  relationship

Explanatory notes

When using this form it is very important that you select a specific example of your problem. The more specific you can be, the better. Then complete the form in the following order.

First, complete C
1. Choose one unhealthy negative emotion from those listed (which could be the main one) and write down the self-defeating behaviour associated with it.
2. Use one form for each emotion if you experienced more than one unhealthy negative emotion in the episode under consideration.
3. If your problem is associated only with self-defeating behaviour, leave the 'emotion' section blank.

Second, complete A

1. Here, it is very important that you focus on the aspect about which you were most disturbed.
2. As it says on the form, it is most important that you assume temporarily that **A** is true. You will have an opportunity later to check on its accuracy.

Third, write down your iBs about A

1. Work from the top of the form to the bottom and complete the relevant sections.
2. Leave blank any section that does not apply.

Fourth, complete D

1. Answer each of the three questions.
2. Don't give a 'parrot' answer. Consider each of your responses carefully and prove to yourself why the correct answer is no.

Fifth, complete rB

1. Work from the top of the form to the bottom and complete the relevant sections.
2. Make sure that you assert the rational belief and negate the irrational belief in each completed section.

Sixth, complete E

1. Provide a healthy negative emotion from those listed, making sure that it is a constructive alternative to the unhealthy negative emotion listed under **C**.
2. Write down your constructive negative behaviour associated with the new emotion.
3. If your problem was associated only with self-defeating behaviour, just complete the 'new constructive behaviour' part of the form, leaving the 'emotion' part blank.

Seventh, reconsider A

While holding the new rational beliefs, go back to **A** and correct any distorted inferences that you find there.

Finally, homework

Discuss a suitable homework assignment with your therapist to strengthen your conviction in your rational beliefs.

A brief reprise

Having given one example of how I train my clients to use a basic REBT skill, let me summarize what a psycho-educational approach to counselling involves. First, the counsellor makes clear at the outset what the approach to counselling that she uses involves, both for her as a counsellor and for the client. This enables the client to decide in an informed way whether or not the approach to counselling practised by the counsellor is likely to be helpful. This is the heart of eliciting the client' informed consent to begin therapy. This approach is in accord with recent thinking in social work (Garvin and Seabury, 1984), which distinguishes between an applicant and a client. When a person first seeks help from a counsellor, he is in the position of an applicant. He becomes a client when he gives his informed consent that he understands what help is to be provided and wishes to take advantage of this help.

Second, it is important for the counsellor to be explicit about the approach to counselling that she practises, emphasizing how it views psychological problems and psychological well-being and how it conceives of the process of therapeutic change. She should judge what her client can understand and provide explanations to him based on that judgement. This spans the entire therapeutic process.

Third, the counsellor is advised to be explicit about the tasks that both the counsellor and the client will carry out during counselling. The more the client learns about the therapeutic approach, the fuller the therapist's explanation will have been.

Fourth, the counsellor teaches the client how to assess his problems and how to use the therapeutic techniques or processes advocated by the approach at hand.

Finally, once the fourth step has been successfully accomplished, the counsellor serves as a consultant to the client for his self-change efforts. In this way she helps him to become his own counsellor.

Personal experiences of being a client
At this point, let me briefly refer to my experience of being a client, as it is relevant. In my mid-twenties, I experienced a low-level depression which I could not shift. As I was undertaking training as a counsellor at that time, it seemed sensible to deal with this issue. So I sought therapy and was referred to a therapist with good credentials. When I first saw him I asked what therapeutic approach he practised. This was met by silence. I then asked him to explain his role, an enquiry that was again met by silence. When I repeated my request (since I naively thought that my therapist may have been hard of hearing), it was met first with an implied question – 'I wonder why this is so important to you' – and when I pushed the issue I was met with an interpretation – 'You seem to want me to feed you'; a response that I found most puzzling. It will come as no surprise that my first therapist was a Kleinian. This episode reveals that I received no education from my first therapist concerning his role, about which I did enquire, and concerning my own role, about

which I did not. How could I then give my informed consent to participate in this therapy? The answer is that I could not. Although I do not have any data to confirm my hunch, I believe that my experience is the norm.

Because I was new to this business of being a client and thought that my experienced therapist knew best (an assumption that most clients make and one that leaves them susceptible to all kinds of abuse), I persisted with his therapy for a number of months, all the time puzzled by his lack of responsiveness.

I quit at this point, not because I was getting anywhere – I was not and still had my low-grade depression – but because I moved.

Then I saw a kindly man who practised a hybrid of psychodynamic therapy and psychodrama. Again I received no proper introduction based on the principle of informed consent. I enjoyed the psychodrama more than the psychodynamic therapy, but got no better.

Then my therapist announced, with proper warning, that he was giving up his practice. I do not think I was responsible for this, but I cannot be sure!

He referred me to a man who taught me a very valuable lesson: how *not* to practise therapy. He neither educated me into my role nor explained about his own; moreover he pathologized my attempts to find out. At the beginning of my eighth session with him, he announced that this was to be my last session with him on the NHS, but that he would continue to see me if I could pay as a private patient. I left in disgust.

Soon after, I read a self-help book entitled *A New Guide to Rational Living*, written by Albert Ellis (the founder of REBT) and Robert Harper (Ellis and Harper, 1975). This book clearly explained to my satisfaction why I was depressed and showed me what I needed to do to stop feeling depressed. I followed this advice and stopped feeling depressed. I resonated with the REBT approach and was able to use it on my own without any outside assistance. It turned out that I became a therapist who has not been helped by being in therapy, but who has helped himself a great deal by practising self-therapy.

Now some might conclude from this that I wish to eradicate therapy and recommend that people should buy a book instead. Nothing is farther from the truth. What I conclude from my experiences is that I was poorly served by my three well-qualified therapists, none of whom took any trouble to educate me about our respective roles. Had they done so, each would quickly have determined that his approach was not right for me and would, I hope, have effected a judicial referral.

Advantages and criticisms of the psycho-educational approach to counselling

The advantages of the psycho-educational approach seem to be the following:

i.   It empowers clients by encouraging them to focus as early as possible on self-change.

ii. Clients can be educated in individual counselling, in small or large groups, and sometimes by the use of self-help material. It is thus an efficient approach to counselling and can reach larger numbers of people than a non-educational approach.

iii. It can guide the construction and implementation of personal and social education programmes in schools and can therefore be employed to prevent the development of problems rather than just approach their remediation.

iv. It promotes peer counselling communities and self-help groups to which the counsellor can serve as a consultant.

Finally, here is a list of some of the criticisms of the psycho-educational approach to counselling, together with my responses:

i.   Clients may resist the psycho-educational approach for a number of reasons. For some it may remind them of being back at school. For others it may seem that their counsellors are trying to make them fit into a pre-existing system.
     Response In using an educational approach to counselling, a counsellor will quickly recognize this and should suggest an appropriate referral . The counsellor should not think that she has to be able to help all those who apply to her for help.

ii. A client may not think of the counsellor as an educator and may want a different kind of relationship with a helper.
     Response Using the educational approach, the counsellor will identify this at a very early stage and refer on.

iii. Some clients may be too distressed or too disturbed to make informed decisions at the beginning of their therapy.
     Response If the counsellor is flexible, she will not burden a distressed client with inappropriate information that he will not be able to process; rather, she will respond to his distress. However, once the distress has receded, the counsellor should

adopt an educational stance. With a very disturbed client, the educational approach can be used, but first the counsellor has to encourage him to stand back and engage with his observational self.

iv. The educational approach to counselling will appeal to administrators, who will see its value in offering intervention for a brief period to large numbers of clients. Counsellors will come under increasing pressure to 'cram in' clients.
Response Both statements may well be true. However, using an educational approach to counselling does not mean that the counsellor has to bow to such pressure. Rather, she needs to educate such administrators in the legitimate and illegitimate uses of the educational approach.

v. Not all counselling approaches lend themselves to psycho-education.
Response True, but all counsellors need to be able to explain their approaches so that applicants for their help can give their informed consent to become clients. All counsellors have something to learn from the psycho-educational approach to counselling.

vi. Therapists who take an integrative approach to their work cannot educate their clients at the outset since they have no way of knowing what blend of approaches they will be taking.
Response Integrative therapists can explain the integrative nature of their work at the outset although this will have to be in broad terms. However, once they have decided on the particular blend of methods they will use with particular clients, there is nothing to prevent them from explaining this blend to their clients. They can then train them to use these methods for themselves.

References
Bannister, D. (1983) The Internal Politics of Psychotherapy. In D. Pilgrim (ed.)*Psychology and Psychotherapy: current trends and issues. London:* Routledge & Kegan Paul.
Dryden, W. *(1995). Brief rational emotive behaviour therapy.* Chichester: John Wiley.
Ellis, A. & Harper, A. *(1975). A new guide to rational living.* North Hollywood CA: Wilshire.

Garfield, S.L. (1994). Research on client variables in psychotherapy. In A.E. Bergin & S.L. Garfield (eds.) *Handbook of psychotherapy and behaviour change* (4th edition). New York: John Wiley.

Garvin, C.D. & Seabury, B.A. *(1984). Interpersonal practice in social work: processes and procedures.* Engelwood Cliffs, NJ: Prentice-Hall.

Maultsby, M.C. Jr (1975). *Help yourself to happiness: through rational self-counselling. New York:* Institute for Rational Living.

Nelson-Jones, R.C. *(1982). The theory and practice of counselling psychology.* London: Cassell.

6

feel better, get worse; feel worse, get better

I delivered this lecture to Obsessive Action, a self help organisation for those who suffer from obsessive-compulsive disorder (OCD) and their families at their day of lectures and discussion groups on October 4, 1997. While I do not specialise in working with those with OCD, I have seen a number of such clients over the years largely due to my professional association with Dr David Veale, a Consultant Psychiatrist working at Grovelands Priory Hospital. In this paper, I outling my views on OCD and how it can be addressed therapeutically from an REBT perspective. The language and tone of the lecture reflect the fact that I was speaking to a lay audience.

I am very pleased to talk to you today, although I do so with some trepidation. Sharing the platform with me is Dr Salkovskis, who is one of the world's leading theorists and researchers in the field of obsessive-compulsive disorder (OCD), and Dr Toates, who is not only a leading psychologist, but knows from first-hand experience what it is like to suffer from OCD and will be drawing on this experience in his talk which follows mine.

When I found out that I would be sharing a platform with such distinguished colleagues, I wondered what tack I should take. I am not a specialist in OCD, although I keep up to date with the research in the area and I have seen a good many clients with OCD in my time. Nor do I suffer, if that is the right word, from OCD, although there are those who know me who claim that OCD really stands for 'obsessive- compulsive Dryden'. Despite this, and although I do own up to some obsessive-compulsive features in my personality, I do not, by any criteria that I know of, suffer from OCD. I should know, since I have checked all the books that have ever been published on the subject fifty-five times!

So what can I offer you today? I offer you some thoughts and insights from the approach to therapy that I practise known as Rational Emotive Behaviour Therapy. This approach to therapy can be located in the cognitive-behavioural tradition, which states that psychological problems can be understood by examining carefully how people think and behave. Now, I do not for one moment wish to imply that OCD can be understood just with reference to the cognitive-behavioural model. I believe that OCD is more complex than that, that it is not just one disorder, but a range of disorders that can be placed under a broad obsessive-compulsive umbrella, and that there are complex psychological and neurological interactions to consider if we are to understand this family of disorders properly.

Today, then, I will attempt to show the contribution that REBT has to make to the psychological understanding and treatment of obsessive-compulsive disorders.

Responsibility and risk appraisal

Currently, there has been much debate in the field concerning the roles that responsibility and risk appraisal play in the genesis and maintenance of certain obsessive-compulsive disorders. In particular, it has been claimed that cognitive distortions of risk appraisal and responsibility for harm at the heart of many obsessions and some compulsions. An example from the field of obsessions is that a person has a thought such as 'I may harm my child' and considers that as a result there is a very good chance of her doing so. Here the appraisal of risk is exaggerated. In addition, the person attempts to avoid all potentially dangerous situations that the child may be exposed to and also attempts either to neutralise the thought (e.g. by saying 'I am a loving mother') or to suppress the thought. These manoeuvres are deemed to stem from an exaggerated sense of responsibility, as shown in the thought, 'If something bad happens to my child then it will be all my fault.'

Why do people develop an exaggerated appraisal of risk and an excessive sense of responsibility? Rational Emotive Behaviour Therapy's view is that these cognitive distortions stem from the person's attitude to safety and to responsibility. REBT argues that this attitude or belief is dogmatic or absolutistic in nature.

Let me give an example from my clinical practice. I have a client, whom I will call Janet, whose problem concerns her fear of harming others who do or may come into contact with her. She has a range of symptoms; thus, she is terrified of contracting Aids – not, I should stress, because of concerns about her own welfare, but because she may infect other people. In addition, if she sees a child at the school where she teaches display an unexplained bruise, she experiences a compulsion to tell somebody in authority about this. Her current preoccupation concerns smoke. She is convinced that she can see and smell smoke in other people's houses and is compelled to bring this to their attention. Finally, she refuses to go on holiday lest she sees unattended luggage which, of course, contains a terrorist's bomb. You will see clearly here the twin distortions of risk appraisal and the responsibility of harm. What is this woman's underlying philosophy concerning risk and responsibility? It is this:

> *'When I am involved, I* must *discharge my responsibility perfectly and it would be terrible if I didn't. If something bad happens, which it is bound to if I do not make absolutely certain that I have done everything I can to prevent it, then this will be all my fault and will prove that I am a thoroughly rotten person.'*

When this belief has been activated in the client's belief system, how will she answer the following questions?

Question: How likely do you think it is that something dreadful will happen if you do not act to prevent it?
Answer: It will definitely happen.

Question: How responsible are you for anything that happens if you do not act to prevent it?
Answer: Totally responsible.

Question: How certain do you have to be about preventing harm to others and about discharging your responsibility?

Answer: Totally certain.

Question: How safe do you have to make it for others who come into
             contact with you?
Answer: Totally safe.

The REBT perspective, I believe, explains why people with OCD see
things related to their problems in black and white terms. As can be
seen from Janet's answers, she holds the following black and white
ideas:

i.   Either something tragic definitely won't happen or it definitely
     will. Here, there is no room for the concepts of possibility and
     probability.

ii. Either I am totally free of responsibility or I am totally
     responsible. Here, there is no room for degree of responsibility
     or shared responsibility.

iii. Either I am certain that harm won't happen or it definitely
     will. Here, the person has no concept that harm may not happen
     if she is not certain. Personal experience of doubt is associated
     in the person's mind with the certainty of harm.

iv. Either things are totally safe or they are dangerous. Here,
     there is no room for slight danger. Because slight danger must be
     eradicated, it becomes extreme danger in the person's mind if it
     cannot be got rid of.

If my client has a predisposition to OCD, which I believe to be the case,
is it any wonder that this absolutistic belief renders her vulnerable to
one of the obsessive-compulsive disorders? I would argue that it is not.
This belief, then, leads her to act in a way that is consistent with OCD
and these actions serve to perpetuate her belief. This mutual
strengthening of belief and behaviour is what makes it so important to
address in therapy both her behaviour and her beliefs. In the past, we
thought that interventions targeted at behaviour would automatically
lead to belief change. We are now older and wiser. We also know from
clinical experience that, if we just target beliefs for change, then the
client may undermine our efforts by continuing to behave in
obsessive-compulsive ways. So, we target both. I argue that we first
need to help the person to develop a healthy, flexible alternative to her
irrational belief. In the case of Janet, here is the belief that we worked
together to construct:

'When I am involved, I want to discharge my responsibility perfectly; but I do not have to do so, nor is it healthy for me to attempt to do so. If I don't do all I possibly can to discharge my responsibility, as I don't have to do, this has advantages and disadvantages and does not mean that something bad will inevitably happen. I can take reasonable steps to prevent bad things from happening without guaranteeing that they won't. If something bad happens as a result, that is very unfortunate, but it is not the end of the world. If it does happen, I will accept my share of the responsibility, which is not total. If I do the wrong thing, I am not a bad person, but a fallible human being who has a responsibility to my own psychological health and happiness as well as a responsibility to take a reasonable amount of care in preventing bad things from happening.'

When this belief has been activated in the client's belief system and she has conviction in it, how will she answer the same questions?

Question: How likely do you think it is that something dreadful will happen if you do not act to prevent it?

Answer: It could happen, but the greater likelihood is that it will not.

Question: How responsible are you for anything that happens if you do not act to prevent it?

Answer: I have responsibility, but others who are involved also have responsibility. There will be occasions when I will have total responsibility, but there will be many more situations when responsibility will be shared.

Question: How certain do you have to be that you have prevented harm to others and discharged your responsibility?

Answer: Reasonably certain, but not totally so.

Question: How safe do you have to make it for others who come into contact with you?

Answer: Reasonably safe, but not totally so.

Janet's rational belief will lead her to be more flexible in her thinking, in contrast to the black and white thinking that stems from her dogmatic, irrational belief. This can be seen in the following:

i. Tragic events do happen, but they are rare and they are not inevitably related to what I do or fail to do. The events that I am concerned with exist along a continuum of probability rather than in two categories labelled 'definitely won't happen' and 'definitely will happen'.

ii. In most cases responsibility can be divided and assigned differentially.

iii. If I am not completely certain that harm won't happen, it does not follow that it definitely will. Events in life are not controlled by my experience of being certain or uncertain. I just don't have that degree of control over events.

iv. Threat and danger can be placed on a continuum where there is room for slight as well as great danger. Danger can rarely, if ever, be eradicated and certainly not by me.

In order for Janet to be really convinced of her rational belief and the flexible forms of thinking that stem from it, she will have to act in ways that are consistent with it. This is a crucial point. It is possible for someone like Janet to understand intellectually that her rational belief is rational, but to continue to act in ways that are consistent with her irrational, obsessive-compulsive disposing belief, in which case her self-defeating behaviour will nullify her rational belief. Given this, it is crucial that her behaviour is in line with her rational belief.

If she follows this latter principle, Janet will have to act against her habitual way of behaving. In doing so she will experience discomfort which, unfortunately, is unavoidable. Consequently, in order to maintain this behavioural-cognitive consistency, Janet will have to tolerate this sense of discomfort. In other words, she will have to tolerate feeling worse in order to get better. If she opts to feel better in the short term by going back to her old behaviour, the purpose of which is to eradicate doubt and risk, she will get worse in the longer term.

In order to sustain and enhance the gains she made through refraining from acting in accord with her irrational beliefs and through choosing to act in a way that is consistent with her rational beliefs, I encouraged Janet to expose herself in a planned way to situations that previously would have triggered her obsessive-compulsive related dogmatic beliefs. Thus, among other activities, Janet agreed to stand in dog shit, wipe it off thoroughly, as any person not suffering from OCD would, and wear the shoes to work while rehearsing her rational belief. She also agreed to go to Heathrow Airport, look for unattended luggage and go home without ascertaining who owned it and without reporting the incident to a member of the airport security staff. She resolved to do such assignments once a week, and although she reported feeling very uncomfortable while undertaking such tasks, she made substantial improvements in her OCD symptomatology.

Gaining control by giving up control

Let me turn my attention to obsessions that are kept alive by the person's attempts to avoid thinking certain thoughts. It is a fact of human life, which is not fully appreciated by those suffering from intrusive thoughts, that as humans (i) we may think various thoughts that are alien to us and (ii) we are limited in our ability to control our thoughts. Indeed, the more we try to banish unwanted thoughts from our mind, the more we are likely to think them.

In this respect, let me tell you about Fiona who has given me permission to tell you her story. Fiona is an orthodox Jewess who in her early twenties had a lesbian dream which she found very disturbing because she thought that this meant that she was a lesbian. Consequently, she tried not to look at women in case she looked at their breasts and private parts. The more she tried not to look at women sexually, the more she did so. Fiona consulted me precisely because I was a man, since by that time she tried to solve her problem by avoiding women as much as possible. Thus, she had stopped travelling by tube because things had escalated to such a degree that she started having intrusive thoughts and images that she would wrestle a woman to the ground and carry out oral sex on her in front of other passengers. Later on in therapy, we would humorously refer to this as the 'assault on the Licktoria Line' incident! Parenthetically, I think that a therapist who works with people with OCD needs to have a good sense of humour.

Fiona's obsessions stemmed from and were kept alive by the following irrational beliefs:

i. I must be thoroughly heterosexual and must not have any thoughts about women of a lesbian nature.

ii. I must be able to control my thoughts perfectly, even in my sleep.

iii. If it turns out that I am a lesbian, which I absolutely must not be, then I am a disgusting person.

iv. If others in my religious community discover that I have been having lesbian thoughts, then they will ostracise me and I could not bear that.

These beliefs led Fiona to try desperately not to have such thoughts, which, as many of you know, is the best way to increase the intrusiveness and aversiveness of unwanted thoughts. This also led her to attempt to avoid contact with people and situations that triggered these thoughts. Again, this is a good way of making it more likely rather than less likely that obsessive thoughts will intrude into the person's mind in the long term.

I first helped Fiona by showing her the crucial role that her irrational beliefs played in the genesis and maintenance of her obsessive-compulsive symptoms. Second, I helped her to construct the following set of alternative rational beliefs:

i. I'd prefer to be thoroughly heterosexual and not have any thoughts about women of a lesbian nature, but there is no law of the universe which states that I must achieve either of these things. Indeed, a person's sexuality is best placed along a continuum rather than in two non-overlapping categories, and if I calm down about my thoughts about women I will be able to be clearer about my sexuality.

ii. I'd like to be able to control my thoughts perfectly even in my sleep, but I don't have to do so. In fact, I now see that desperately trying to control my thoughts will only lead to an increase in such thoughts rather their elimination.

iii. If it turns out that I am a lesbian, which I would prefer not to be, then this certainly does not prove that I am a disgusting person. Rather, it proves that I am a fallible human being who would prefer to be heterosexual.

iv. If others in my religious community discover that I have been having lesbian thoughts and ostracise me, then I would really find it difficult to tolerate this, but I could bear it. If this happens, then I can make a life for myself in a more liberal Jewish community.

Fiona came to see that these rational beliefs were consistent with reality, logical and healthy and that her irrational beliefs were false, illogical and unhealthy, but she fully recognised that she needed to work towards really believing them. This work involved Fiona allowing herself to think lesbian thoughts and to have lesbian images while practising her rational beliefs. She was to do nothing to eliminate or reduce the frequency of these thoughts and images. She was to wait until they passed through her mind no matter how long this took.

After doing this, Fiona began to confront situations which she had previously avoided and to practise her new set of rational beliefs while doing so. For example, she spent a day going up and down the Victoria

Line sitting next to and directly opposite women and standing close to them in the rush hour.

All this work left Fiona feeling worse in the short term, but helped her to get better in the longer term. She made great strides in therapy, and a year after we had finished therapy, she rang to tell me that she had lost her virginity to a man she had been dating for about six months who, believe it or not, happened to be a trainee rabbi!!

REBT's contribution to the understanding and treatment of OCD in a nutshell

Let me now make a few general remarks about REBT's contribution to the understanding and treatment of OCD.

   i. REBT holds that at the psychological core of most forms of OCD lie a set of rigid and extreme beliefs about certain key themes such as responsibility, threat and control. These beliefs are known as irrational beliefs because they are false, illogical and unhealthy. There are four such beliefs:

      i) Demandingness (which takes the form of 'musts', absolute 'shoulds', etc.)

      ii) Awfulising (e.g. 'It's awful, terrible or the end of the world that...')

      iii) Low frustration tolerance (e.g. 'I can't stand, tolerate or bear it')

      iv) Self-deprecation (e.g. 'I am bad, defective or worthless')

   ii. These irrational beliefs lead to the cognitive distortions often found in OCD. Thus, they help to explain why people with OCD greatly overestimate risk to themselves and to others and why they take complete responsibility in situations where objectively responsibility is shared.

   iii. These irrational beliefs and the cognitive distortions that they help create also explain the overt and subtle cognitive and behavioural manoeuvres that people with OCD undertake to try to deal with their problems, but which serve only to perpetuate them. In short, these manoeuvres are designed to help you feel better but in fact help you to get worse.

   iv. A person can, through understanding and a dedication to hard work, change these irrational beliefs and learn a much healthier set of rational beliefs (which takes the form of healthy preferences, anti-awfulising, high frustration tolerance and self-acceptance). This work involves a non-OCD rehearsal of these rational beliefs, confronting previously avoided situations and the client's willingness to let herself think whatever she thinks without neutralisation and other attempts to control her thinking. This work will lead the individual to feel worse in the short term, but will help her to get better in the longer term.

If I were to sum up REBT's perspective on OCD in a nutshell it would be this. OCD is maintained by your attempts to feel better, which only lead you to get worse. Therapy involves you doing things that will lead you to feel worse, but will help you to get better. So, if you all feel worse at the end of this talk, I will be very pleased!!

7

rationality and Relate

I delivered this lecture at the AGM of the Wimbledon and Merton office of Relate on July 3, 1997. As I note in my lecture, I used to be a Marriage Guidance Counsellor and took the invitation to talk as an opportunity to reflect upon my current thinking on couple counselling.

My experiences with Relate

I used to work for Relate – or, more accurately, I used to work for your organisation when it was known as the National Marriage Guidance Council. This was back in the early 1980s when I was looking to work more extensively with couples. I was at that point fully trained as a Rational Emotive Behaviour Therapist, but in order for me to offer my services to the local centre, which incidentally was Birmingham, I had to go to Rugby for training. So off to Rugby I went for marriage guidance counsellor training, which at that time comprised a mixture of theoretical sessions and discussion groups which focused on our personal reactions to the material and to each other. What it didn't do was to teach us about how to work with couples in a practical way. I understand that matters have since changed, but, not being *au fait* with current training at Rugby, I couldn't possibly comment.

Apart from insisting that I attend training at Rugby, which they were obliged to do, Birmingham Marriage Guidance allowed me to practise couple counselling in my own way – i.e. as a Rational Emotive Behaviour Therapist – and, while they supervised me in a general manner, they had no objection to my seeking specialised REBT supervision elsewhere. This involved making audiotapes of counselling sessions, which I was allowed to do as long as my clients gave their informed consent.

This state of affairs continued happily until I moved to London in 1985. My wife, who also was a marriage guidance counsellor (doesn't it feel good to hear that phrase again!) and I decided that we wanted to continue to work for the MGC and applied to London. We met with Renate Olins, but were not accepted by the London MGC because we were not prepared to offer three evenings per week to the organisation: we could only offer two. This brought to an end my career as a Marriage Guidance Counsellor. Sadly, I never did become a Relate counsellor.

Actually, I wrote a formal letter of complaint to Rugby about London's inflexibility, but received a reply which in essence said 'London do their own thing; we have no control over them.' That was in the days before London declared UDI.

I recently had an experience which reminded me of London's inflexibility and would like to share this with you. One of my REBT trainees is a trained Relate counsellor and wanted to receive supervision from me on his REBT work with couples. His supervisor at Relate was adamant that he could not tape his sessions, and that was the end of that. This contrasted with Birmingham's more flexible, encouraging attitude fifteen years earlier.

I mention these incidents to you, first, to show you that I have been part of the organisation in which you work and, second, to highlight what I see as the ambivalent attitude that Relate has towards diversity of counselling approach. For, while I have heard representatives of the organisation say that they would welcome outside practitioners from a variety of different approaches, when it comes to it they back away from creating opportunities to allow this to happen. I was fortunate to encounter a local centre which encouraged me to bring my REBT skills to couple work. My trainee and others that I have met have been less fortunate.

You may be thinking at this point that you would be against the practice of allowing Relate counsellors to tape record their counselling sessions. However, if the reasons for the use of audiotapes are explained to clients and they are given an opportunity to decline their use, then in my opinion there is no valid argument against this practice. After all, it was Carl Rogers who pioneered the use of audiotapes in counselling, and if it was good enough for Rogers, it should be good enough for Relate.

Couple dissatisfaction and couple disturbance

Having got that off my chest, let me turn my attention to the contribution that Rational Emotive Behaviour Therapy has to make to work with couples. REBT argues that each partner in a couple brings to the relationship a number of preferences about (i) aspects of the relationship, (ii) their partner and/or (iii) themselves in the relationship. Problems begin both when these preferences aren't met and/or when the two people have incompatible desires. In REBT theory, these problems come under the heading of couple dissatisfaction, in that one or both people in the relationship are dissatisfied when their preferences are not met. This is why it is so important for people to be as honest as possible with themselves and with their potential partners about their true preferences with respect to relationships, so that both people can make informed choices about their commitment to a long-term relationship. This is also why it is important that the focus of premarital counselling should be on helping engaged couples to discover and share with one another their true desires about married life.

In general, the more important the desire, the greater the dissatisfaction when that desire is not met. However, dissatisfaction on its own does not usually lead to destructive couple discord. What tends to lead to such discord, or what REBT theory calls 'couple disturbance', is when one or both partners transform their *desires* into absolute *demands* about (i) aspects of their relationship, (ii) their partner and/or (iii) themselves in the relationship.

These demands, which are often couched in the form of musts, have to's, got to's and absolute shoulds, lead to a whole range of unhealthy negative emotions which partners experience when their demands are not met. When your clients tell you that they experience anxiety, depression, unhealthy anger, shame, guilt, hurt, jealousy and unhealthy envy, this is a clue that they have one or more relationship-oriented demands which are not being met.

While this is the core of the REBT view of couple disturbance, the situation is far more complex than this. Thus, people often act in self-, partner- and/or relationship-defeating ways, either to stop themselves from experiencing unhealthy negative emotions in the first place, or to get rid of these emotions once they have started to experience them. In addition, people can act in ways that are consistent with their unhealthy negative emotions and the beliefs that underpin them, and these actions are more often than not also self-, partner- and/or relationship defeating. Add to this the tendency of partners to locate their emotions in the behaviour of the other, rather than in the *beliefs they hold* about the behaviour of the other, and what do you get? You get the fact that dealing with couples' problems is frequently a very complex business.

The desire for active counselling and practical learning

Over the years I have seen many couples who have come to me in my private practice after seeking help from Relate counsellors. Since I routinely ask all my clients about their previous experiences of counselling, I have discovered two sources of dissatisfaction about Relate counselling. First, many of my ex-Relate couples have said that their counsellors were too passive to be helpful. These counsellors either kept quiet while the partners rowed or encouraged the couples to talk to one another, which in many cases was an invitation to row even more. Second, these couples complained that they did not learn anything that was of *practical* use to them at Relate. This latter theme crops up time and time again.

Now I am enough of a scientist to be sceptical of these impressions. They are taken from an unrepresentative sample and a fairly small one at that. But it does echo what Pat Hunt (1985) found just over a decade ago in her study of client experiences of Relate counselling.

My personal view is that counsellors cannot afford to be passive when they work with couples. If they are, they will fail to model one crucial quality that many partners in disturbed couple relationships lack: the skill of focusing on disturbed interactions and on the issues that underpin them. This focusing skill is a prelude to understanding the factors involved and to learning how to deal with them in more productive ways. By and large, you just cannot wait and hope that couples will do this for themselves. No, as counsellors you have to intervene actively and help your couples to create a space where they can focus on their problems long enough to understand and deal with them. My view is that the more successful Relate counsellors do this. It will come as no surprise to you to learn that REBT therapists are active in this way as a matter of course.

However, creating a focus is not therapeutic on its own. What is therapeutic is what the partners learn about themselves within that focused space: not just any old learning, but learning that can make a real difference in their lives. I am speaking of learning that can help both partners deal productively with their disturbed emotions and the dysfunctional interactions that are closely associated with these emotions. This is not to say that my couple clients claimed that they learned nothing from their Relate counsellors. Far from it. Many of them stated that they learned how their current problems had roots in their past. But, and I want to emphasise this, they claimed that this learning was not practical enough either to help them change how they felt, or to help them change how they acted towards one another. Again, I do not want to overplay this. I am referring to an unrepresentative, small sample, but nevertheless these people have something important to say. They are saying that they value insights that they can use in their everyday life. May I modestly point out at this juncture that this is the kind of learning that REBT couple counselling endeavours to facilitate.

The counsellor's tasks in REBT couple counselling
So how do I as an REBT couple counsellor work? The best way that I can explain this is to outline eight tasks that I perform in working with couples. While I will outline these tasks in the most logical order, I wish to state at the outset that in practice the order of these tasks is quite flexible and fluid.

Task 1: Understanding the problems
First, like any other couple counsellor, I ask the partners to tell me about their reasons for seeking help and what they would like to achieve from counselling. In doing so, I steer quite carefully between giving the couple an unfettered opportunity to express themselves and helping them to keep to the point. While listening to them, I formulate hypotheses which I test out by asking the couple questions, the answers to which help me to reject any hypotheses that are disconfirmed.

During this opening period I also make notes, mainly of the problems that the partners are expressing. I do this because I find it helpful to encourage the couple to develop a problem list. This is effectively a list of problems the partners wish to address in counselling. Since it is important, in my view, for counselling to be goal-directed as well as problem-focused, I also help them to develop a goal for each expressed problem.

I agree with those couple counsellors who say that it is also helpful to encourage couples, as early as possible, to focus on their strengths as a couple as well as on the areas of conflict between them. I too like to do this in the early phase of couple counselling, but if it seems that a particular couple is a long way from considering this issue, I do not press the point.

Task 2: Giving a thumbnail sketch of rational emotive behavioural couple counselling and eliciting informed consent to proceed

One of the principles that I hold dear in the field of counselling is that known as informed consent. With respect to counselling, the principle of informed consent states that it is important for counsellors to explain to clients, in ways that are likely to be understood by the clients, the nature of the approach to counselling that they practise. The purpose of this explanation is to help clients make up their minds whether or not to proceed with this particular approach to counselling.

At this stage, the explanation that I give is likely to be brief, but it does need to inform. Typically, I explain to my couple clients that the approach to couple counselling that I practise involves helping them to understand why they have problems and what they can do to address these problems. In doing so, I explain that I will help them to focus on their beliefs about their relationship, their partner and themselves in the relationship. I explain that unhealthy beliefs are at the core of many couples' problems. I continue by saying that holding healthy beliefs helps partners to communicate and solve problems more effectively, while holding unhealthy beliefs leads to communication breakdown and an increase in couple conflict rather than its effective resolution. I mention that I am also willing to teach them a range of skills as appropriate and at the right time.

I then ask the couple whether or not what I have said makes sense to them. If so, I ask them whether or not they wish to proceed. If not, I answer any questions the couple may have and elaborate on any points that may be unclear, and then I ask them whether or not they wish to proceed. I stress to the couple that my goal at this point is to give them a thumbnail sketch of my approach and that I will explain more about my approach as we proceed. If it transpires that a couple prefers a different counselling approach, I endeavour to effect a suitable referral.

Task 3: Teaching the distinction between couple dissatisfaction and couple disturbance

If a couple gives their informed consent to proceed, my next task as an REBT couple counsellor is basically an educational one. It is to teach the couple the REBT model of couple dissatisfaction and couple disturbance. I do so by following a number of steps in sequence.

First, I ask both partners independently what they want from the relationship, what they want from the other person and what preferences they have of themselves in the relationship.

Second, I ask both partners to indicate to what extent their desires are being met in each of the three aforementioned areas.

Third, I ask them to indicate how they feel and respond in each of the areas where their desires are not being met. At this point I introduce the concept of healthy and unhealthy negative emotions. I show them that, in general, the following emotions are both negative and unhealthy: anxiety, depression, unhealthy anger, shame, guilt, hurt, jealousy and unhealthy envy, and that the following emotions are both negative and healthy: concern, sadness, healthy anger, disappointment, remorse, sorrow, concern for one's relationship and healthy envy. I help the couple to see that the latter emotions are healthy alternatives to the former.

I also show the couple, in some detail, that unhealthy negative emotions tend to lead to self- and relationship-defeating behaviour and distorted negative thinking, while healthy negative emotions tend to lead to self- and relationship-enhancing behaviour and realistic thinking. I then ask them to return to their list of thwarted desires and ask them to indicate whether they are responding to each with a healthy negative emotion or an unhealthy negative emotion.

Fourth, I take the issues where one or both partners are experiencing an unhealthy negative emotion and ask whether or not this emotion helps the person to address constructively the issue on which their desire is thwarted. Invariably, the couple can see that unhealthy negative emotions lead to couple conflict and discord and do not in any meaningful, long-term way help them deal with the issue of their thwarted desires.

Fifth, having established that unhealthy negative emotions lead to conflict and discord in the couple and that these emotions prevent effective problem-solving of thwarted desires, the next step is to encourage the couple to deal with their unhealthy negative emotions. I explain that the initial focus of Rational Emotive Behavioural couple counselling will be on helping them to change these emotions to their healthy negative equivalents.

At this point, you may be thinking what some of my couples put into words: that I am helping partners in a couple to feel bad. This is, in fact, exactly what I am trying to do. My initial aim is to help partners to feel healthily bad about not getting their important desires met. I don't want them to feel good about this, nor do I want them to feel indifferent about it. I want them to experience healthy negative emotions because (i) it is realistic and healthy for them to do so and (ii) these emotions will motivate them to have meaningful, productive discussions about how they can address the issue of their thwarted desires. As one couple insightfully put it: 'You want us to feel bad about the state of our relationship, whereas we have been feeling miserable and disturbed about it.'

Put more technically, if I have been successful at this stage, I have helped the couple to see that we need to focus on issues of couple disturbance before we can productively deal with issues of couple dissatisfaction. I believe that much couple counselling goes awry either because counsellors attempt to help their couple clients deal with issues of couple dissatisfaction without helping them to address and overcome couple disturbance issues, or because they try to deal with both at once.

Task 4: Teaching the ABCs of couple disturbance and couple dissatisfaction

My fourth task is also an educational one. Having explained the difference between couple disturbance and couple dissatisfaction and helped both partners to use this model to understand their problems, I proceed to help them to understand that underlying their healthy negative emotions is a set of rational or healthy beliefs and underlying their unhealthy negative emotions is a set of irrational or unhealthy beliefs.

Using a particular episode in which both partners (rather than just one of them) experienced unhealthy negative emotions, I teach them the ABCs of couple disturbance. In doing so, I show them one at a time that their disturbed feelings are largely determined by one or more of the following unhealthy beliefs: rigid musts, awfulising beliefs, low frustration tolerance beliefs and beliefs where they deprecated themselves, their partner and/or the relationship. By using the same episode, I show them that, if they were to hold the rational alternatives to these irrational or unhealthy beliefs, they would experience healthy distress about the event and this would help them to deal with the event more productively. These healthy or rational beliefs take the form of: flexible preferences, anti-awfulising beliefs, high frustration tolerance beliefs, and beliefs where they accepted themselves, their partner and/ or the relationship.

Task 5: Teaching partners how to dispute their irrational beliefs

This fifth task involves teaching the couple to dispute or challenge their irrational or unhealthy beliefs. I generally do this by questioning the empirical, logical and pragmatic basis of these beliefs. In doing so, I make sure that I dispute each partner's unhealthy beliefs in a given session. If I challenge only one partner's unhealthy beliefs in a session, that partner may fel that I am siding with their partner against them or they may think that I view them as the sick one in the relationship and their partner as the healthy one. So, even if I succeed in only partially challenging both partners' irrational beliefs in a given session, this is preferable to disputing one partner's unhealthy beliefs fully.

The goal of disputing is twofold. First, I strive to help partners see that their irrational beliefs are inconsistent with reality, are illogical and yield unhelpful results. Second, I strive to help them understand that their rational beliefs are consistent with reality, are sensible and yield helpful results which are realistic, given the negative event that we are analysing, (see Dryden, 1995).

Task 6: Helping partners to weaken their conviction in their irrational beliefs and to strengthen their conviction in their rational beliefs
Helping partners to challenge their irrational beliefs *once* is insufficient to promote meaningful belief change. Such change involves partners *repeatedly* challenging their own irrational beliefs and practising the rational alternatives to these beliefs. REBT has many different techniques to aid this process. Basically, we have a host of cognitive, imaginal, emotive and behavioural techniques that we can teach clients to help them to weaken their conviction in their irrational beliefs and strengthen their conviction in their rational beliefs (see e.g. Dryden, 1995; Ellis et al., 1989).

Task 7: Dealing with couple dissatisfaction
This penultimate task involves helping couples to address their dissatisfaction about their relationship. For reasons that I have already discussed, this task is best done once both partners have made progress at overcoming their disturbed unhealthy negative emotions about their thwarted desires. There are a number of ways of addressing issues of couple dissatisfaction, and the ones chosen will depend on what form the dissatisfaction takes.

Common methods of dealing with issues of couple dissatisfaction include:

i. empathy training – where partners complain that they do not "feel" understood by the other;

ii. communication training – to encourage partners to take responsibility for and to own their own feelings in their communications to one another;

iii. assertiveness training – to encourage partners to express their negative feelings in constructive ways and to express their positive feelings whenever possible;

iv. negotiation training – to encourage each one to get more of what they want from the relationship while helping their partner to get more of what they want also;

v. problem-solving – where partners have difficulty solving practical and emotional problems;

vi. effective relationship management – to help couples spend more quality time with one another;

vii. tolerance training – to help partners agree to differ and to tolerate what cannot be changed in their relationship;

viii. attributional training – to help partners make healthy attributions about each other's behaviour;

ix. training in good parenting skills; and

x. sex therapy training.

I wish to stress that the above is only a partial list, but it will give you a flavour of what REBT couple counsellors do in this phase of the work.

As you can tell, the emphasis here is on good relationship skills and these skills are tailored to the individual styles of the partners concerned. However, as appropriate, the focus of the work returns to belief change when it becomes apparent that one or both partners have unhealthy beliefs that will otherwise interfere with the skills-based work that is characteristic of this phase of couple counselling.

Task 8: Promoting relationship actualisation

The final task that I wish to discuss here is one that counsellors either do not offer or that couples do not avail themselves of. This task involves the counsellor helping a couple to strive towards maximising the potential in their relationship. When couple counselling is effective, couples often leave happy with the gains that they have made, particularly when they look back and recall the conflictual state of their relationship before they came to counselling. However, either they do not realise or their counsellors do not bring to their attention the fact that they can have an even better relationship.

Relationship actualisation work focuses on helping couples to identify what they ideally want from their relationship and to encourage them to work towards realising these lofty goals. Love has been defined as an emotional and psychological state which occurs when one partner meets the deepest desires of the other. Couples who sustain love at this deep level are fully committed to meeting the deepest desires of the other and are prepared to take active steps to do this. While I believe that it is inhuman to expect couples to do this consistently for one another, the happiest couples do reach these peaks reasonably often. If, as counsellors, we do not offer such work to our clients, we are shortchanging them at the last hurdle.

I hope I have given you at least an idea of what REBT couple counselling is like. Perhaps it is a pipe dream, but I would like to see REBT training offered on the Relate curriculum, not as the dominant counselling method, but as an option for those counsellors who want an alternative to the current training fayre. If tonight I have planted a seed, maybe Wimbledon and Merton MG can provide the soil and the water for the seed to flower.

References

Dryden, W. (1995). *Brief rational emotive behaviour therapy.*
    Chichester: John Wiley.

Ellis, A., Sichel, J.L., Yeager, R.J., DiMattia, D.J., & DiGiuseppe, R.
    (1989). *Rational-emotive couples therapy.* Elmsford, NY:
    Pergamon Press.

Hunt, P.A. (1985). *Clients' responses to marriage counselling.* Rugby:
    National Marriage Guidance Council.

8

why I do not help my clients to raise their self-esteem

This lecture was given on October 9, 1997 to the Department of Psychology at the University of east London as part their Invited Speakers Programme. As most of the audience were likely to be interested in counselling psychology, I decided to speak on Rational Emotive Behaviour Therapy's unusual stance on self-esteem.

It doesn't take trainee counsellors long to discover that many of their clients suffer from low self-esteem, for low self-esteem lies at the bottom of many psychological problems. It would seem logical, therefore, if one of the primary goals of counselling were to help clients raise their self-esteem. While this may seem a sensible and non-controversial objective for counsellors, I will argue in this talk that pursuing this seemingly laudable objective is fraught with problems and dangers and, if I am right, counsellors would do well to re-think this whole issue before going along with the crowd on this point.

What I will do in this lecture is, first, consider to what extent low self-esteem underpins clients' psychological problems. Second, I will take a close look at the concept of self-esteem and outline some of its difficulties. Finally, I will outline an alternative method of helping clients raise their self-esteem which will render them less vulnerable to relapse. It will come as no surprise to those who are acquainted with some of my writings that my thesis is informed by the theory and practice of Rational Emotive Behaviour Therapy (REBT), an approach to counselling that falls squarely in the cognitive–behavioural therapeutic tradition and that I have been practising now for twenty years.

The role of low self-esteem in clients' problems
As I mentioned above, problems to do with low self-esteem can be found across the whole range of problems for which clients seek help. Whichever way you wish to categorise these problems, self-esteem is lurking in the background. Sometimes however it is very much in the foreground, and may in fact be the first thing that your client mentions. How many times has a client said to you at the very beginning of therapy: 'My problem is that I suffer from low self-esteem' or 'I guess it all boils down to the fact that I don't like myself very much'?

If we take the major disturbed emotions that clients keep referring to in counselling, we again find the omnipresence of low self-esteem. For example, many anxiety problems can be attributed to a person's perception of threat to her self-esteem; in depression, a person may be preoccupied with his unworthiness and the fact that he is a failure; in guilt, a person considers himself bad for breaking or not living up to his moral code, and in shame, a person considers herself to be defective, for example when she falls short of her ideal, particularly when this occurs in public.

I do not mean to imply that we can completely account for clients' problems by referring to the concept of low self-esteem, for this would be a gross oversimplification. Indeed, quite a few client problems have more to do with non-ego issues than with ego issues. Nevertheless, such is the frequency with which low self-esteem, in all its different forms, crops up in counselling that it deserves close critical scrutiny.

The concept of self-esteem

If we are to help clients to raise their levels of self-esteem, it would be useful if we first understood what it is that we are attempting to help raise. In other words, what exactly is self-esteem? The REBT answer to this question involves defining the terms 'self' and 'esteem'. Paul Hauck (1991), a noted REBT therapist and writer, defines the 'self' as 'every conceivable thing about you that can be rated'. Now, what can be rated about a person? Let me answer this question with reference to Arnold Lazarus's (1989) modality view of humans.

Lazarus argues that you can assess people and their problems in the following seven modalities: behaviour, affect, sensation, imagery, cognition, interpersonal relationships and physiological and bodily functioning. Using this framework, we can say that the self must include the following:

i.   all the behaviours that a person has performed in his or her lifetime;

ii. all the emotions that the person has ever felt;

iii. all the sensations that the person has experienced;

iv. all the images, dreams and fantasies that the person has had;

v.   all the thoughts and beliefs that the person has had;

vi. all the interactions with other people that the person has had;

vii. all aspects of the person's physiological and bodily functioning.

To which can be added: the person's characteristics and traits and their various talents, skills and abilities.

The term 'esteem' comes from the verb 'to estimate', which means to rate, evaluate or judge. The question then is: can we legitimately rate the 'self'? Clearly, the REBT answer to this question is a resounding 'no', because, as we can see from Hauck's definition and what follows from it, the self is far too complex to be rated. In addition, even if we could rate the person after discovering and rating the billion pieces of data gathered under the above headings, as soon as we had done so, the rating would be out of date because the person would have changed and produced more data in each category.

Thus, the self is not only too complex to be rated, it is constantly in flux and you cannot legitimately give a static rating to a constantly changing phenomenon.

Why raising self-esteem is problematic

Whenever I have asked a person who suffers from low self-esteem what would raise her self-esteem, on most occasions the person says something like: 'a better figure, more friends, being more interesting to people, being more successful at work, a better career, more money', etc. Indeed, the list is endless. However, if the person were magically given the missing ingredient, this would emphatically *not* solve that person's self-esteem problem. REBT argues that this is so for the following reasons:

Self-esteem is conditional

Let's suppose that Janet believes that she is less worthy without a partner than she would be with a partner. Now clearly, if she does not have a partner she will think badly of herself. And if she meets a partner she will think better about herself. However, even if Janet has a partner, her belief will lead her to experience a lot of anxiety because she has the idea that she would be less worthy again if she lost her partner. This is an example of conditional self-esteem, where a person's self-esteem fluctuates according to whether she has or doesn't have something that she values.

Conditional high self-esteem is fleeting

Let's suppose that Janet meets someone special. Operating on her belief that she is more worthy if she has a partner than if she is without one she begins to think and feel better about herself. Her self-esteem has been raised because she has met a new partner and she believes that she is now worthwhile as a person. However, she is still vulnerable to emotional disturbance because it is very likely that she places additional conditions on her self-esteem. Thus, she may think that she will be a failure if she does poorly at work. So if she then gets a very poor appraisal at work, because of her work-related belief she will think that she is a failure. Her increased worth that has come about through meeting a new partner is not sufficient to sustain her self-esteem.

Human beings are frequently more preoccupied with what they do not have than with what they have. Thus, if we are in good health we take this for granted and hardly give it a thought. But if we become ill, we suddenly become preoccupied with the state of our health. When we return to full health, we may for a while give thanks that our health has been restored, but this awareness of our good health will not last long. Similarly, when Janet does not have a partner and believes that she is less worthy as a result, she will be preoccupied with her lack of a partner and with her lack of self-esteem. When she does have a partner in her life, she will temporarily focus on the fact that she has what she values in her life and that her self-esteem has been raised; but she will soon adjust to this new state of affairs, and when she experiences a lack in some other area of her life to which she attaches her self-esteem, she will become preoccupied with this lack and with the accompanying decrease in her self-esteem. This is why conditional high self-esteem is fleeting.

Self-esteem involves two ratings when one will suffice

When Janet does not have a partner in her life and she believes that this makes her less worthy than when she does have one, she is in fact making two ratings or evaluations. First, she is rating the lack of a partner in her life negatively; but then she goes on to evaluate her 'self' negatively. Janet's lack of a partner is discrete enough to merit a rating and, indeed, it is healthy for her to rate this lack negatively. For if she did not do so then she would not be motivated to do something about it. However, her rating of her entire 'self' is needless, for three reasons. First, as we have seen, it is empirically inconsistent with reality, since Janet is far two complex to be given a global rating. Second, it is very poor logic for Janet to conclude that not having a partner in her life means that her worth as a person is diminished. Third, Janet's conclusion that her worth as a person is diminished if she does not have a partner does not help her at all. In fact, this conclusion may well lead to greater misery for her in the long term. For her belief that her worth is diminished if she does not have a partner may well lead her to try desperately to find someone to be her partner – and we all know how successful being desperate is in helping us to find a suitable long-term mate. So when Janet does have not have a partner, she benefits from rating number 1, i.e. rating the lack of a partner negatively. However, she largely suffers from rating number 2, i.e. rating her 'self' negatively as a result.

What happens when Janet finds a soulmate and is still operating on the idea that her worth is dependent upon having a partner? Once again, she makes two evaluations. First, she wisely and healthily evaluates positively the presence of a partner in her life. This makes sense because it reflects Janet's values and preferences and it leads her to experience pleasure and satisfaction. But then, unwisely – and, we would argue in REBT, unhealthily – she evaluates herself positively. This second evaluation is problematic even though it is positive. It is problematic for the same reasons that Janet's negative self-evaluation when she did not have a partner is problematic. First, it is inconsistent with reality. We can prove that it is good for Janet to have a partner in her life, but we cannot prove that this makes her a worthier person. Indeed, she has not changed: the only thing that has changed is her partnered status. Second, it is illogical. For Janet to conclude that the worth of her 'self' has increased because she now has a partner is as illogical as her conclusion that the worth of her 'self' is diminished when she is without a partner. Third, it does not help Janet to believe that her worth has increased when she has a partner, precisely because this situation may change in the future. As we have already seen, her conditional belief that she is more worthy with a partner than without one leaves her vulnerable to anxiety when she thinks that it is possible for her to lose him. It also leaves her vulnerable in other ways. Thus, she may experience jealousy when her partner speaks to another woman because her underlying low self-esteem leads her to think that the other woman is more attractive and more interesting than her and that her partner will see this and will prefer to be with the other woman. Additionally, given her underlying low self-esteem, Janet may be prepared to tolerate bad behaviour from her partner and be very reluctant to end her relationship with him. Low self-esteem is a major reason why people are prepared to tolerate abusive behaviour from partners, since they feel that any relationship, however bad, is better than no relationship at all.

Self-acceptance: REBT's preferred alternative to self-esteem

If REBT therapists do not encourage their clients to raise their self-esteem, what do they do instead? In a phrase, they encourage their clients to work towards self-acceptance. What does this involve? Let me answer this question from my own practice by outlining six steps.

First, having helped my client to see the drawbacks of self-rating, I explain what self-acceptance is. I help the client to understand that the "self" is unrateable, complex, in flux, fallible, and unique. Accepting oneself means acknowledging this fact. While all humans are unrateable, complex, in flux and fallible, I stress that it is the quality of uniqueness that distinguishes one human from another. This uniqueness is based on the idiosyncratic combination of many different aspects and means that an individual cannot be replicated. Even if we could clone a person, her clone will differ from the original in a variety of respects.

Second, I underline that self-acceptance encourages the person to rate different aspects of herself and to rate her experiences, but it discourages her from assigning a global negative rating to herself as a whole. I stress that refraining from rating oneself is not something that one can do easily, and certainly one cannot do it perfectly, since self-rating comes relatively easily to human beings (Ellis, 1972). As Neenan (1997) has said, it is more realistic to help clients to achieve greater self-acceptance than to achieve full self-acceptance.

I go on to explain to the person that rating aspects of herself is helpful because it alerts her to what she needs to change in herself. In contrast, self-rating discourages the person from changing negative aspects of herself because it focuses her attention on her global negativity rather than on her specific negative aspect.

Third, I stress that unconditional self-acceptance allows the person to see herself in a very broad context. It helps her to take a realistic view of her strengths and weaknesses. If the person adopts a self-esteem perspective, she is automatically biased when viewing these strengths and weaknesses. Thus, when she is judging her "self" negatively (i.e. when she has low self-esteem), she is likely to see many more weaknesses than strengths. The weaknesses that she lists will be very negative while any strengths that she lists will be moderate or mild. Therefore, the person is likely to overestimate her weaknesses and underestimate her strengths.

On the other hand, when the person is judging herself positively (i.e. when she has high self-esteem), the opposite is likely to occur. In other words, she is likely to list more strengths than weaknesses, and the strengths that she lists will be very positive while her weaknesses will be moderate or mild. Thus, the person is likely to overestimate her strengths and underestimate her weaknesses.

However, when the person accepts herself unconditionally, she will tend to list strengths and weaknesses in equal measure, and the valence of these strengths and weaknesses will be evenly distributed. This, I would venture, is the most realistic of the three types of self-judgement outlined.

Fourth, I explain that adopting an attitude of unconditional self-acceptance increases the chances that the person will make accurate, realistic inferences about the activating events that she focuses on, while an attitude of self-esteem will lead to the formation of biased inferences.

When the person has low self-esteem (i.e. when she evaluates herself in a global negative way), she is likely to make inferences about reality that are distorted and exaggerated in a negative direction. These inferences are likely to be examples of what cognitive therapists have called cognitive distortions. For instance, the person may magnify the negative aspects of a situation and minimise its positive aspects. On the other hand, when the person has high self-esteem (i.e. when she evaluates herself in a global and positive way), her inferences are likely to be characterised by positive illusions. For instance, the person may minimise the negative aspects of a situation and maximise its positive aspects.

By contrast, when the person accepts herself, her inferences are likely to be realistic and non-distorted. They are likely to be balanced and to incorporate both the positive and negative aspects of a situation. This is one reason why healthy thinking is more conducive to good mental health than positive thinking.

Fifth, I demonstrate that self-acceptance and self-esteem are likely to affect the person's behaviour differentially. Thus, when the person has low self-esteem will inhibit healthy risk-taking and promote avoidant behaviour, whereas high self-esteem will promote ill-considered risk-taking and grandiose behaviour. Self-acceptance, on the other hand, encourages healthy risk-taking and constructive behaviour.

Finally, I explain to my client that conditional self-esteem tends to stem from a rigid philosophy of demandingness where the person insists that he must get what he wants or that he must not get what he does not want. REBT theory posits that this philosophy is at the core of much psychological disturbance. Unconditional self-acceptance, by contrast, is deemed to stem from a flexible, preferential philosophy where the person has a clear idea of what he wants and what he doesn't want, but where he recognises both that he does not have to get what he wants and that he is not immune from getting what he doesn't want. REBT theory holds that this flexible, preferential philosophy lies at the core of psychological health.

Thus, if a person believes that he must succeed in business, then he is likely to think poorly of himself if he doesn't do well (which is the low self-esteem position), and he is likely to think well of himself if he does do well. Consequently, he will tend to live a kind of yo-yo existence where his worth and his emotions go up and down depending on the conditions that currently exist in his life.

However, if the person wants to do well in business but does not believe that he *must* do so, then he will tend to accept himself unconditionally whether he does well or does poorly in this area of his life. This flexible, preferential philosophy will enable him to feel good about his success on the one hand and bad about his failure on the other, but it will stop his worth as a person from rising or falling accordingly.

At this point you may be wondering what is wrong with high self-esteem, since it has positive benefits. While this is the case, it is important to distinguish between positive benefits and healthy benefits on the one hand, and short-term benefits and long-term benefits on the other.

First, the positive benefits of high self-esteem may not be healthy. I stressed that high self-esteem leads a person to overestimate his strengths and underestimate his weaknesses. While this may help to generate positive feelings, it gives the person a false picture of himself and may lead him to think that he is doing better in life than he actually is. Thus, he may be unprepared when he confronts grim reality on this point. Also, high self-esteem doesn't help him to focus on his weaknesses and to improve those aspects of himself that need improving.

Furthermore, the above benefits are short-term in nature and tend not to endure. Thus, you cannot have high self-esteem without being vulnerable to low self-esteem since they are opposite sides of the same belief coin. Therefore, if you think that you are worthy because you have a partner (the high self-esteem position), you will also think that you are less worthy if you are without a partner (the low self-esteem position). So, if your client wants the benefits of high self-esteem, he will also have to accept the costs of low self-esteem. There is, however, one way in which a person can have high self-esteem and not suffer, and it is to this point that I now turn.

Unconditional positive self-esteem: the other alternative

Unconditional self-acceptance is the preferred REBT alternative to conditional self-esteem because it discourages the person from rating himself and because it advocates that when the person accepts himself he does so unconditionally; i.e., the person is advised to accept himself no matter what. Some clients, however, *want* to rate themselves. If I am not able to dissuade them from doing so, I will implement REBT's other alternative to conditional self-esteem. This is known as unconditional positive self-esteem and involves the person considering himself to be worthwhile and to base his worth on conditions that do not change. These conditions are: (i) that he is a fallible human being, (ii) that he is unique, and (iii) that he is alive. As can be seen, the person will always be fallible, always be unique and will remain alive until he dies. So a person who believes 'I am worthwhile because I am human, unique and alive' will not get into trouble emotionally. This shows that the real problem with conditional self-esteem is its conditionality, as when a person believes, say, that he is worthwhile *as long as* he is successful.

However, as Ellis (1972) has said in his seminal article on self-acceptance, unconditional positive self-esteem is problematic because it cannot be proven. Thus, a person could believe 'I am *worthless* because I am human, unique and alive', and this belief is equally unprovable. Unconditional self-acceptance, on the other hand, with its emphasis on an *acknowledgement* of who we are rather than on an *evaluation* of who we are, is amenable to proof. It is for this reason that most REBT therapists prefer the unconditional self-acceptance solution to the unconditional positive self-esteem solution, but will accept the latter when for one reason or another the client is not prepared to implement unconditional self-acceptance.

The importance of *teaching* unconditional self-acceptance

REBT therapists adopt an educational approach to helping clients develop self-acceptance. We believe that we can teach clients both the principles that form the philosophy of self-acceptance and a variety of techniques that can be used by them to deepen their conviction in this philosophy between sessions. This educational emphasis is in direct contrast to the approach adopted by person-centred therapists, for example, who hold that the client can develop an attitude of unconditional positive regard if she experiences the therapist's unconditional positive regard for her.

The main difference between the REBT position and the person-centred position here concerns the importance of the educational phase. This phase plays little or no role in person-centred practice (PCP) where the focus is predominantly on the quality of the relationship between client and therapist. In PCP, during the therapeutic process the client learns that her therapist respects her unconditionally and begins to learn as a result that she is a person worthy of regard. As Patterson (1974) has shown, once the client learns to regard herself unconditionally, she can learn to regard others in the some way and, more importantly, can demonstrate this attitude to others. When these others experience the client's regard for them, they can reciprocate in kind; the whole tone of the client's relationships with others then begins to be characterised by mutual regard, and this helps to sustain the client's regard for herself.

I have several reservations with this position. First, the client's regard for herself tends to be conditional upon her experiencing the therapist's regard for her. She does not learn that she can accept herself even if the therapist does not have regard for her.

Second, I question whether the developing attitude of mutual regard between the client and her significant others, facilitated as it were by the client's own self-regard, occurs as frequently as Patterson claims. Thus, it is more than possible that in some cases the client's attempts to show others respect will be exploited by those other people for their own selfish ends. How many times have you heard clients complain that their good treatment of others has not been reciprocated or has been used against them?

This leads me to my third criticism of the person-centred position: namely, that it does not help clients specifically enough to accept themselves in the face of rejection and betrayal from others.

Finally, even if the scenario put forward by Patterson does occur, can this effect be attributed to the client's experience of the therapist's regard for her? This has not been demonstrated.

REBT does not deny the importance of the therapist's acceptance of the client in the therapeutic process, but it argues that the long-term therapeutic potency of REBT self-acceptance therapy lies in the client's understanding of the principles of self-acceptance and putting this philosophy into practice many times in her own life. Unless the therapist teaches the client these principles, and stresses that repeated practice of them is crucial, the client may either not learn the principles of unconditional self-acceptance or not put them into practice of her own accord.

In REBT, we also argue that when the client experiences the therapist's acceptance this leads her to *feel* better, but on its own it will not lead her to *get* better, by which I mean to develop a solid self-accepting attitude which she can sustain when the going gets tough. On the other hand, when the client commits herself to practising the principles of unconditional self-acceptance in her own life, and does so repeatedly over time, this practice helps her both to feel better and to get better. This proposition does however, await empirical inquiry, which in turn depends on the development of an adequate measure of unconditional self-acceptance.

In this talk, I have explained why REBT therapists do not try to help clients raise their self-esteem. Instead, we try to encourage them to develop and practise an attitude of unconditional self-acceptance. I appreciate that this is a contentious issue and that many of you may disagree with me. If you do not agree with me, that will be bad; but I will continue to accept myself as a unique, unrateable, complex, fluid, fallible human being.

References

Ellis, A. (1972). *Psychotherapy and the value of a human being.*
    New York: Institute for Rational-Emotive Therapy.
Hauck, P. (1991). *Hold your head up high.* London: Sheldon Press.
Lazarus, A. (1989). *The practice of multimodal therapy* (update).
    Baltimore: Johns Hopkins University Press.
Neenan, M. (1997). Reflections on two major REBT concepts.
    The Rational Emotive Behaviour Therapist, 5 (1), 31-33.
Patterson, C. (1974). *Relationship counselling and psychotherapy.*
    New York: Harper & Row.

9

influence your clients for their health's sake: a rational emotive behavioural perspective

I delivered this lecture at a conference entitled 'Power and Influence in Psychotherapy' on November 15, 1997. The conference, which was held at the University of London School for Oriental and African Studies (SOAS), was organised by the Universities Psychotherapy Association (UPA). This lecture marks the first occasion that I ever asked to speak at a conference having seen the original panel of speakers and lecture titles. I took this unusual step because I thought that it was important that the views of a cognitive-behaviour therapist were represented at such an important conference.

There are many ways of viewing the role that psychotherapists adopt in the endeavour known as psychotherapy. Thus, therapists have been seen as facilitators of their clients' personal development (Mearns & Thorne, 1988), as friends from whom their clients purchase friendship (Schofield, 1964), as co-voyagers on a spiritual journey, as confessors who receive their clients 'shameful' revelations, or as blank screens on whom patients (this time) project their unresolved transferences and with whom they act out their unresolved conflicts.

While some of you may object to one or more of the above roles, it is likely that these ways of conceptualising the role of the psychotherapist are likely to be viewed far more favourably than the roles that I will consider in this lecture. The roles of psychotherapist that I will be discussing here today are those of influencer and teacher.

The idea that the major role of the therapist is to influence the client is unpopular for two major reasons. First, 'influence' conjures up notions of brainwashing and cults where unscrupulous therapists influence clients for their own benefit rather than for the client's benefit, and do so in a way that encourages and, in some notable examples, forces clients to suspend their critical faculties so that they go along with the therapist's views just because they *are* the therapist's views. Therapists who influence their clients in this way – and fortunately such unscrupulous practitioners are in the minority – often suffer from a sense of inadequacy and a need to have devoted disciples to feel powerful and gain a sense of importance. They are often dogmatists and believe that they have *the* truth, and others have to go along with them to sustain their fragile egos. When such practitioners come to light they give influence a very bad press, and other more ethical therapists tend to view all attempts to influence clients as malevolent. I will argue in this lecture that this opinion is misguided and will put forward the view that influence, far from being a dirty word, is therapeutic when it is done ethically with due regard for a client's autonomy.

The second reason why influence is viewed negatively by therapists is that it threatens their self-image; they prefer to see themselves as benign facilitators whose major task is to provide a certain set of therapeutic conditions in which the healthy part of the client can flower and blossom. You will, of course, recognise the views of Carl Rogers (1957) and person-centred therapists from this description. The idea that therapists should deliberately influence their clients rather than establish and maintain a therapeutic climate does not 'feel right' to many therapists, who prefer to see themselves as companions on their clients' journey towards self-actualisation. An interesting paper published in the mid-1960s showed, however, that even Rogers was subtly influencing his clients by the differential use of minimal encouragers to talk. Rogers was shown to say 'mm-hmm' when his clients engaged in a certain type of talk and to withhold the same when they engaged in another type of talk. The effect was that his clients more often engaged in the reinforced type of talk than in the non-reinforced type (Truax, 1966). I am sure that Rogers was unaware of this form of influence, and therein lies the danger. It is my view that unaware attempts to influence clients are more abusive than explicit attempts. In the latter, therapists are open about what they are trying to do and they elicit their clients' informed consent to be so influenced. If such consent is not obtained, ethical therapists abandon their attempts to influence their clients and talk openly with them about alternative ways forward.

What I will do in the remainder of this talk is to describe how I explicitly and openly attempt to influence my clients to adopt a perspective on emotional problem-solving, and how I do this in a way that safeguards their autonomy. Before I do so, I wish to point out that there is an impressive body of literature that demonstrates that when therapy is effective clients adopt their therapists' values, and when it is not effective they fail to adopt these values. This effect has been termed 'value conversion' by Tjeltveit (1986) in an important review paper which repays careful reading.

In short, whether we like it or not, and whether we admit to it or not, as therapists we do influence our clients. Given this fact, my point is: let us do so as explicitly and ethically as possible. If we adopt the safeguards that I will now describe, we will be using our power is a non-abusive way.

Pre-influence considerations: teaching the REBT framework and outlining client and therapist tasks

One of the reasons why therapist influence on clients is a matter of concern is because of the ethical issues that such influence raises. My view is that the influence that I strive to exert over my client is ethical for two main reasons. First, this influence is in my client's interests and not in mine. If I succeed in influencing my client to apply in her life the principles and techniques of Rational Emotive Behaviour Therapy – which is the approach to therapy that I practise – then, I hypothesize, *she* will benefit. The only way *I* will benefit (apart from receiving a professional fee) is from the satisfaction of helping the client to live a more fulfilled life.

Second, my influence is ethical because I explain to the client the specific ways in which I will be trying to influence her and I will attempt to influence her in these ways only if she gives her informed consent for me to do so. As the *Code of Conduct, Ethical Principles and Guidelines* of the British Psychological Society states, 'Psychologists shall normally carry out . . . interventions only with the valid consent of participants, having taken all steps to ensure that they have adequately understood the nature of the intervention and its anticipated consequences' (BPS, 1997: 2).

In this section, I will describe the manner in which I explain to prospective clients how REBT conceptualises client problems and, broadly speaking, what tasks REBT expects the client and the therapist to carry out over the course of therapy. I want to stress at the outset that, when the therapist gives such explanations, he or she does so while keeping very much in mind the ability of the client to understand these explanations, and with due respect to the appropriate timing of these explanations. It is not the case that when a person comes in for the first time I bombard him with a lot of explanatory information: rather, I ask what he is seeking help for and respond therapeutically to what he has to say. In doing so, I look for suitable opportunities to explain about REBT and associated client/therapist tasks.

I want to reiterate that this is done within the context of this therapeutic response, so that I can understand if what I have to say sounds mechanical and overwhelming for the client. In reality, however, in the hands of a skilled, sensitive REBT practitioner it is neither. This is an important issue, a full discussion of which lies outside the scope of this paper.

Teaching the REBT framework
As I have just mentioned, I am a practitioner of REBT. As such, my initial task is to explain to people who seek my help how I am likely to conceptualise their problems. There are various ways in which I do this. Thus, I may ask the person to give me a specific example of one of her problems and explain to her what factors I think are important to consider in understanding her problem; in particular, I will show the person the role that irrational beliefs play in her problem. Second, I may take a general example of the client's psychological problems and again explain to her my view that at the core of this problem lie one or more irrational beliefs that account for the existence of this general problem. Finally, I may choose to teach the person a general model of psychological disturbance in which irrational beliefs are deemed to play a central, determining role. Whichever teaching method I use, I am careful to point out to the person that my way of conceptualising problems is but one of many that exist in the psychotherapeutic domain, and that if my approach does not make sense to her then I am happy to refer her to a therapist whose view is more congruent with her own.

To take a stark example, many years ago I was consulted by a man who rang me and asked me if I practised RT. Now REBT was known at its inception as Rational Therapy or RT, and although I found it a little odd that the person was referring to REBT by its previous initials I thought no more about it. When I met the person I outlined the REBT model of psychological disturbance, to which my client reacted with incredulity. It turned out that he thought I practised Reichian Therapy. I did not attempt to persuade this client to my way of thinking, even though I am personally highly sceptical of Reichian Therapy; rather, I referred him to a local practitioner of that approach to psychotherapy.

This episode raises the following important and interesting question: when does a person who seeks your help become your client? For me the answer is: when the person understands my therapeutic approach, understands what this approach will, in broad terms, require of us both and, based on this understanding, gives his or her informed consent to proceed. Until the person has given such consent, he or she is best regarded as an applicant rather than as a client; after the person has given such consent, he or she becomes a client.

Like other approaches to psychotherapy, REBT has a decided perspective on psychological disturbance and health. REBT's view of psychological disturbance is that at its core lie the following set of rigid and extreme beliefs:

i. Demandingness (believing that one must get what one wants or must not get what one does not want).

ii. Awfulising (believing that it is the end of the world if negative activating events occur and that nothing could be worse).

iii. Low frustration tolerance (believing that one cannot tolerate negative events which are difficult to tolerate).

iv. Depreciating self, others and the world (believing that oneself, others and the world can be legitimately given a single negative evaluation, and rating oneself, others and the world negatively when one's demands on self, others and the world are not met).

On the other hand, REBT argues that at the core of psychological health lie the following alternative rational beliefs:

i. Holding non-absolute preferences (believing that, while it is desirable to get what one wants and not to get what one does not want, neither of these states is essential).

ii. Anti-awfulising (believing that it is bad if negative activating events occur, but it is not the end of the world if they do; things could always be worse).

iii. High frustration tolerance (believing that one can tolerate negative events that are difficult to tolerate and that it is worth doing so).

iv. Acceptance of self, others and the world (believing that oneself, others and the world cannot be legitimately given a single negative rating, and acknowledging, when one's desires are not met, that oneself and others are unique, complex, ever-changing individuals with a mixture of positive, negative and neutral aspects, and that the world is a complex place in which one sometimes has one's desires met, but not inevitably so).

After I have outlined this perspective and checked with my client that she has understood the differences between these two sets of beliefs, I ask her the following question:
'Which of these two sets of beliefs would you teach your children, and why?'

Almost invariably, clients respond that they would teach their children the set of rational beliefs, because these are much healthier than the irrational beliefs. I then ask my client another important question:
'Which set of beliefs would you like me to help you acquire and why?'

When the person indicates that she wants me to help her acquire the set of rational beliefs, because these beliefs will help her to overcome her psychological problems and be healthier for her, then I consider that I have gained her informed consent to proceed to influence her in the interests of enabling her to acquire these beliefs.

Outlining client and therapist tasks
I then give the prospective client an outline of the tasks that both she and I are likely to carry out in REBT. In his tripartite reformulation of the psychoanalytic concept of the working alliance, Bordin (1979) argued that 'tasks' was one of the three components of the alliance, and that effective therapy is chracterised by therapist and client understanding their own and the other's tasks and agreeing to carry out their respective tasks; in addition, engaging in these tasks should lead the client to achieve her goals and enable her clearly to see the link between carrying out these tasks and achieving her goals.

I explain to the prospective client that as an REBT therapist I will carry out the following tasks:

i. I will initially focus on the client's problems one at a time and help her to identify the irrational beliefs that lie at the core of her problems.

ii. I will then help the client do two things: (a) question her irrational beliefs and understand why they are false, illogical and unhelpful, and (b) question her rational beliefs and understand why they are true, sensible and helpful.

iii. I will follow this up by suggesting various tasks that the client can undertake to strengthen her conviction in her rational beliefs and weaken her conviction in her irrational beliefs.

iv. I will help the client to identify, challenge and change her core irrational beliefs (defined as irrational beliefs that the client holds in a large number of problematic situations) and to acquire and strengthen a set of alternative core rational beliefs.

v. Throughout this process, I will help my client to voice her doubts and reservations about the process of REBT and to disclose obstacles to carrying out her tasks, and I will deal with these as appropriate.

vi. Finally, I will teach my client a number of other cognitive behavioural techniques relevant to her situation which she can use to prevent relapse and to maintain, broaden and enhance her therapy-derived gains.

I also explain that, if the person becomes a client of mine, it is likely that she will be asked to do the following:

i. at the beginning, discuss specific examples of her problems and help me to assess them using the ABC framework of REBT;

ii. learn to assess her problems using this ABC framework;

iii. join me in questioning her irrational beliefs and their rational belief alternatives;

iv. learn how to question these beliefs for herself;

v. learn and practise a variety of techniques designed to help her to weaken her conviction in her irrational beliefs and strengthen her conviction in her rational beliefs;

vi. generalise her gains by acting in a way that is consistent with her core rational beliefs;

vii. voice her doubts and reservations about the process of REBT and discuss her obstacles to carrying out her tasks.

In conclusion, a person becomes my client when three conditions, related to the content of REBT, are met:

i. The person understands REBT's perspective on psychological disturbance and agrees that she wishes to acquire rational beliefs.

ii. The person understands, in broad terms, the tasks that REBT expects of her and agrees to carry out these tasks.

iii. The person understands, in broad terms, the tasks that REBT expects of her therapist and agrees to proceed in therapy in the knowledge that the therapist will carry out these tasks.

Influence compromises in the process of REBT
My experience is that, if I have explained to the client at the outset how REBT is likely to conceptualise her problems and what our respective tasks are, then REBT will proceed more smoothly than if I have not given my client such explanations.

As therapy proceeds, my influence attempts are as outlined above in the tasks that I have as an REBT therapist. To reiterate, I attempt to influence my client by having her use REBT's ABC assessment framework, by challenging her irrational beliefs and by encouraging her to adopt and act in ways that are consistent with her rational beliefs. In short, all my influence attempts are to get my client to adopt and apply REBT to her own life.

Throughout this process and at every opportunity, I make explicit the basis for my interventions and elicit my client's cooperation. When this is not forthcoming, I am willing to make a number of compromises in my attempts to influence the client. Thus, negotiation between client and therapist in REBT occurs not only at its outset, but throughout the entire process.

Let me now consider one important area of compromise. REBT theory argues that self-rating is problematic and is at the root of self-esteem problems, particularly when it is conditional (e.g. 'I am worthwhile *if* I do well'). According to REBT theory, the healthiest alternative to conditional self-rating is unconditional self-acceptance, because this position does not involve self-rating at all. However, another 'less elegant', but still acceptable, alternative to conditional self-rating is unconditional positive self-rating, where the person rates himself as worthwhile, for example, but does so unconditionally. In effect, he is saying, 'I am worthwhile because I am human, alive and unique.'

My practice is to outline the principles of unconditional self-acceptance and unconditional positive self-esteem to my client, stressing as I do so the advantages and possible disadvantages of each concept. But what if the client, having listened to and understood my explanations, still wants to operate according to the position of conditional self-esteem and considers her worth to vary according to her achievement (for example): how would I respond? My own practice is to reiterate the disadvantages of this position and the advantages of the other two positions, but I would respect my client's decision to adopt a solution that (according to REBT theory) still leaves her vulnerable. I would work within the client's paradigm and help her to be as healthy as I could within a potentially unhealthy paradigm.

I would compromise the REBT position here for three reasons:

i. to do otherwise would threaten the working alliance;

ii. while I might check from time to time whether the client would be willing to change her mind on this issue and adopt one of the other two healthier positions, to disregard the client's view and continue to persuade her to adopt a position that she clearly does not wish to adopt would be an abuse of power and of one's position as a benevolent influencer;

iii. the compromise does not pose a serious mental health risk for the client. If the compromise *did* pose a serious risk for the client and the client would not shift her position, I would stop working with her and effect a suitable referral (normally psychiatric). I should add that this is a rare occurrence and is a last resort.

Other compromises are less controversial and usually concern how ambitious the client is prepared to be in carrying out homework assignments. I may suggest, for example, that a client carry out a particular assignment three times a day, but she may initially wish to do so only once a day. Rather than immediately accede to the client's wishes, I would explain why I was asking more from her and suggest a compromise where she would carry out the task twice a day. As my mother used to say, 'If you don't ask, you don't get.' However, if you ask for a compromise and you don't get it, don't threaten the working alliance: go along with your client.

Let me review my position at this point. As an REBT therapist, I have a clear idea of what would be helpful to the client. I will explain this position and review its advantages and possible disadvantages. I will not impose the REBT preferred position on the client and will frequently make compromises with this position with clients who do not wish to adopt the REBT view. In making such compromises, I will still check from time to time to see if the client is prepared to change her mind on this issue, but again I wish to stress that I would not unilaterally impose my position on the client. If the client wishes to adhere to a belief that is harmful for her, then I will be quite clear about why I consider it harmful and will reserve my right to discharge the client if worse comes to worst. I should add that this latter scenario has not yet happened to me in twenty-two years' practice, but if it did I would endeavour to place the client in an alternative treatment facility.

Some dangers of using influence in REBT

If therapist influence in REBT has the potential for helping clients, it also has the potential for harming them. In this section I will consider briefly the potential hazards of such influence.

Unfortunately, unscrupulous therapists exist in all orientations, and in the hands of an unscrupulous REBT practitioner therapist influence can cause a lot of damage. Thus, an REBT therapist who seeks to be the powerful head of a cult may encourage his or her clients and disciples to use REBT mindlessly and dogmatically for the ego-aggrandizing effects that having a devoted but suggestible following may bring. Although REBT discourages clients from uncritically and mindlessly accepting the word of an authority just because that person *is* an authority – even an authority on REBT – some of its practitioners who seek an adoring following may flout this important principle and create an oppressive environment where questioning or challenging the views of the therapist is not allowed.

Aside from this scenario, therapist influence in REBT may be harmful when the therapist holds a number of irrational ideas that may lead to the dogmatic practice of REBT. Thus, a therapist who believes that he (in this case) must be right may influence clients to adopt a view that is incorrect, although the therapist thinks it is correct. Thus, the therapist may opine that the client holds an irrational belief about achievement which the client may not, in fact, hold. Believing that he must be right, the therapist may foist this view on to the client and brook no opposition. The client is in fact persuaded to accept an invalid position and learns that she has to accept the therapist's view just because it *is* the therapist's view. This state of affairs is not only potentially harmful, but can also be said to be abusive. What is lacking here is therapist humility, where the therapist considers his views to be hypotheses about reality which need to be tested against reality and confirmed or disconfirmed by the client, instead of pearls of truthful wisdom handed down by the infallible oracle.

A second harmful example of therapist influence occurs when the therapist believes that his own self-worth depends on his making progress in therapy. This may result in the therapist persuading the client to state that she is making more progress than she actually is. Thus, the therapist may induce the client to claim that she holds rational beliefs which she does not actually hold. The therapist may also influence the client to withhold her doubts and reservations about REBT and to conceal her problems from him because she intuits that he is threatened by the reality of her continuing problems. To ensure that the client is not influenced by what may be called pernicious REBT, the therapist needs to challenge and change the idea that he *must* help the client make progress and that he is an inadequate person if he doesn't.

Finally, the situation can arise in which a client is harmed because the therapist fails to influence him when it is healthy and in the client's long-term interests to be influenced. When an REBT therapist fails to influence the client appropriately, it is frequently due to the therapist's belief that she (in this case) needs the client's approval. Thus, rather than run the risk of challenging the client's irrational beliefs because doing so may temporarily discomfort the client, the approval-needing REBT therapist backs off from making these challenges. The result is that the client may feel better and think that the therapist is kind and caring, but may get worse (or at least will make no real progress) because he has not challenged and changed his irrational beliefs, which remain firmly in place.

An REBT therapist who, conversely, does not believe that she must have her client's approval will not back off from disputing the client's irrational ideas or from debating with the client whether such ideas are true or false, logical or illogical and healthy or unhealthy, even though the client may be discomfited during this debate and may consider the therapist temporarily harsh and uncaring. Effective REBT therapists do not see therapy as a popularity contest; rather, we recognise that it is, at times, an uncomfortable experience for the client, but that gain often does come not without pain; and we continue to influence the client even when the going gets rough. Needless to say, effective REBT therapists carefully monitor the strength of the working alliance and may back off from influencing the client if doing so will threaten this alliance to the point of rupture. In short, effective REBT therapists are more concerned with how effective they are being than with how positively they are thought of by their clients.

Conclusion
In conclusion, let me state that I regard the effective practice of REBT as ethical persuasion. It is persuasive in that I am attempting to persuade my clients to adopt a healthy philosophy towards themselves, other people and the world. It is ethical in that I am completely open about what I am trying to do and why I am trying to do it, and in that I elicit

my client's informed consent to be persuaded before initiating the persuasive process. It is also ethical because I am prepared to compromise on my preferred REBT strategy and, will with very few exceptions, work to help my clients become as healthy as they possibly can be within their paradigms when this is different from my preferred paradigm.

Let me close on a personal note. I sought individual therapy in my mid-twenties for a low-grade depression. For various practical reasons, I saw three different therapists over an eighteen-month period, but derived little help from any of them, although all three were very experienced practitioners of their art. Not one of them explained to me how they practised therapy or invited me to give my informed consent to proceed. If they had, I would have probably decided not to work with them because, as I figured out later, their ideas about what was effective in therapy were very different from mine and there was little scope for a useful rapprochement. I am not sure whether they thought that explaining how they worked would deleteriously affect the work that they did with me, or whether they simply thought that they knew best and my place was to go along with them because they were the experts. The point is that I didn't know what they practised or how they practised, and that was the problem.

Some of the people who consult me may think that REBT is nonsense, or worse, dangerous. But at least they know what its basics are before they commit themselves to becoming clients. The fact that my therapists told me nothing about their practice meant in effect that they were attempting to influence me with their interpretations and other procedures in the absence of my informed agreement to be influenced. This, I put it to you, is the real danger of influence in psychotherapy.

References

Bordin, E.S. (1979). The generalizability of the concept of the working alliance. *Psychotherapy: Theory, Research and Practice*, 16, 252-260.

British Psychological Society BPS(1997). *Code of conduct, ethical principles & guidelines.* Leicester: BPS.

Mearns, D., & Thorne, B.J. (1988). *Person-centred counselling in action.* London: Sage.

Rogers, C.R. (1957). The necessary and sufficient conditions of therapeutic personality change. *Journal of Consulting Psychology*, 21, 95-103.

Schofield, W. (1964). *Psychotherapy: the purchase of friendship.* Englewood Cliffs, NJ: Prentice-Hall.

Tjeltveit, A.C. (1986). The ethics of value conversion in psychotherapy:

appropriate and inappropriate therapist influence on client values. *Clinical Psychology Review,* 6, 515-537.

Truax, C.B. (1966). Reinforcement and non-reinforcement in Rogerian psychotherapy. *Journal of Abnormal Psychology,* 71, 1-9.

10

why self-help books
don't work

I gave this talk on November 28, 1997 at the Eastbourne branch of
Waterstones bookshop to commemorate the publication of my latest
self-help book (*Overcoming Shame,* Sheldon Press, 1997). It represents another mark of my affection for Eastbourne. As you will see
when you read the chapter, the seeming contradiction between the title
of the lecture and the public relations nature of the occasion is not as
stark as the title of the talk suggests.

You may think it peculiar that I am addressing you tonight on the subject of why self-help books don't work when I am celebrating the publication of my latest self-help book. Is this a cheap publicity stunt? Have I just made the terrible realisation that I have wasted my time writing about a dozen self-help books and am about to atone for my errors? Or have I just gone mad?

I can assure you that that this is not a cheap publicity stunt and I am, as far as I can judge, in the pink psychologically. And yes, I *do* still think that self-help books are valuable aids to mental health. So why do I say that self-help books don't work? Indeed, precisely what do I mean when I say that they don't work?

Recently, I suggested to one of my clients that he read my self-help book entitled *Ten Steps to Positive Living* (Dryden, 1994). This book is a general text, based on the approach to counselling that I practise known as Rational Emotive Behaviour Therapy, and it outlines the REBT view that people have psychological problems because of the rigid and extreme beliefs that they hold about events. It also explains how people can identify, challenge and change these beliefs so that they can live more fulfilled lives.

At his next counselling session, my client said to me: 'I've read your self-help book, but it doesn't work.' The way that he phrased his remark gave me food for thought and the following dialogue ensued.

Windy: What do you mean by it didn't work?
Client: Well, I read what you had to say and it made perfect sense, but I didn't feel differently after I finished it.
Windy: But did you do any of the exercises that I suggested in the book?
Client: Well, I had a go at one or two, but they didn't help much.
Windy: How much time did you devote to the exercises?
Client: Oh, about a couple of minutes.
Windy: So let me get this straight. You read my book and it made sense to you and you spent a couple of minutes doing the exercises that I suggested in the book, but that at the end of all this you didn't feel any better. Is that right?
Client: That's exactly so.

Effectively, what this client was expecting was to read my book and to feel better immediately with the very minimum of effort. He was demonstrating elements of two major attitudes which almost guarantee that the person who holds these beliefs will derive little lasting benefit from self-help books and the exercises that they recommend. These attitudes are:

i. All I need to do to benefit from a self-help book is to read it.

ii. I can derive benefit from any self-help exercise that the author suggests with a minimum of effort.

While many people when confronted with these attitudes will deny that this is what they believe; nevertheless, they act on these attitudes. So, effectively, this is what they actually believe. Let me take a closer look at these attitudes.

Reading self-help books is sufficient to effect change

Occasionally, I come across people who have a large number of self-help books in their library. This is particularly the case with books that purport to help you lose weight. The idea such people seem to have and act on is that all you have to do to effect personal change is to read what an expert has to say about change. This is rarely, if ever, the case. Passively reading a self-help book will only give you cognitive insight into the nature of the problem being written about and the way the author suggests that you need to approach this problem in order to overcome it.

Now, I am not knocking passive reading or the insight it generates. You need to read a self-help book to judge whether or not what the author has to say about the problem and how to tackle it makes sense to you. If it does not, then by all means cast the book aside. However, if it does make sense to you, then it is important for you to fully appreciate that the insight you have gained is necessary for you to take the next step, but is insufficient for you to effect the desired change.

Half-hearted action is sufficient to effect change

Not everyone believes that all you need to do to effect change is to passively read a self-help book. Indeed, most people, when asked, will say that change involves putting a set of procedures into practice. However, people who try a set of procedures that they have read about in a self-help book and quickly conclude that these procedures do not work are usually acting on the idea that half-hearted action is sufficient to effect change. Again, I want to stress that these people will often deny that they hold such an idea; indeed, they may claim that they *know* that half-hearted action will not produce lasting change. Nevertheless, and this is the important point, they act as if they believe it.

Half-hearted action, again, rarely if ever produces a meaningful, lasting change. The reason for this is that change involves repeatedly going against ingrained habits and habitual ways of thinking, and doing so means thinking and acting in ways that are foreign to the person. In other words, change involves making a decision to commit oneself to taking repeated measures which are difficult and uncomfortable to take. Is it any wonder, then, that half-hearted attempts to change will bear no fruit?

Self-help books and the search for magic

When my client, whom I discussed above, claimed that my self-help book didn't work, although he agreed with my approach and the measures that I suggested in it, he was operating as if he believed in magic. He did not realise this and would deny it if I put it to him, but nevertheless this is what his statement amounts to. For the idea that passively reading a book and taking half-hearted action on the principles outlined in that book will lead to long-lasting personal change is just that – a belief in magic.

Let me put it this way. Let's suppose that you have a personal problem that you want to address and you attend a convention where several people are talking about their approach to personal change. At one stand, one of the speakers is advocating an approach to change that is quick, easy, comfortable and involves little or no effort on your part. All you have to do is to listen to a set of audiotapes twice a day for two weeks and your problem will be solved. I am on another stand, saying that change is a difficult, lengthy process and involves putting up with discomfort and making a sustained effort. Which of these two approaches to personal change would you be drawn to? My guess is that in your head you would know that my approach was probably the right one, but in your heart of hearts you would hope that the other speaker was right. You might even buy a set of the tapes that the speaker was peddling – just in case.

It is this 'just in case' type of thinking, this clinging on to the slight hope that after all there just might be a quick, painless and easy way to change, that is so seductive and so powerful here. It is magical in nature, of course, and thus in all probability untrue, but you never know ... The 'just in case, you never know' attitude is one of the reasons why people keep buying self-help books, in the hope that this latest book will lead them to the holy grail.

The trouble is that sometimes reading a self-help book *can* lead to a dramatic change, For example, on reading a self-help book you may clearly understand something that you have been puzzled about for a long time, or you may try a technique that really seems to help. However, such dramatic change does not last without the sustained work necessary to maintain it.

The nature of personal change

Let me now outline how I conceive of the process of personal change.

Step 1. Acknowledge that you are largely (but not completely) responsible for your emotional destiny

This is one of the hardest steps for people to grasp and fully implement. We are far more used to blaming our feelings on other people (e.g. 'You made me so angry') or on situations ('Not getting job the really depressed me') than we are to acknowledging that it is the way that we think about events that largely determines how we feel and act.

There are two other reasons why we are reluctant to accept responsibility for how we feel. First, we may think that doing so means that the way people treat us and the situations that we face are irrelevant to how we feel. This is certainly not true. Just because the way we think about events determines the way we feel more than the events themselves, it does not mean that these events are unimportant. My colleague Paul Hauck has put this well when he says that how we are treated by others and the situations we encounter account for up to 49 per cent of how we feel and act towards these events. We are thus responsible for the other 51 per cent.

The second reason why we eschew responsibility for our feelings is that we may blame ourselves for the important part that we play in creating our own psychological problems. If taking responsibility means blaming ourselves, then, faced with either doing this or blaming other people or situations, it makes sense to do the latter. However, taking responsibility does not mean that we have to blame ourselves. Responsibility means saying: 'I did it and that was bad, but I'm not a bad person. I'm a fallible human being who did the wrong thing. What can I learn from this?' Blame, on the other hand, means saying: 'I did it and that was bad and I am a bad person for acting in the way that I did.' This shows that accepting responsibility does not have to involve self-blame.

In summary, this first step in the change process is perhaps the most important step of all. It involves your acknowledging that you create, to a large degree, your own psychological disturbances and that, while environmental conditions contribute to your emotional problems, they are in general of secondary consideration in the change process.

Step 2. Acknowledge that you have the ability to solve your emotional problems

This second step is important because, if you do not think that you have the capability to solve your emotional problems, then you will not make the necessary effort to change. This lack of effort, in turn, will not produce the changes that you would ideally like to make, which is, of course, a self-fulfilling prophecy.

The main way to tackle obstacles to this step involves doing two things. First, you need to ferret out the precise reasons why you think that you are not capable of changing. For example, do you think you are too old to change, or too set in your ways? Do you think that are too disturbed to change or that you come from too dysfunctional a background to be able to help yourself? The real change-blocker in all these views is the word '*too*'. Yes, you may be advanced in years and you may be set in your ways, but this doesn't have to pose an insuperable obstacle to solving your emotional problems, given the right tools and the commitment to use them. But, add the word 'too' and you won't try to change, and as a result you won't change. So watch out for the word 'too' when it comes to this step and realise that it is just not true. The factors to which you attach the word 'too' may explain why you may find making a personal change difficult, but they do not, in general, explain why such change is impossible to achieve. Add the word 'too', and you make it impossible.

The second thing that you need to do is test out your idea that you are *too* old to change. For example, set yourself a realistic target and work towards achieving it, but do so without constantly reminding yourself that you are *too* old to change. Keep an open mind about this point, or even repeat to yourself that you are *not* too old to change. I know of cases where people in their nineties have made a significant personal change. If they can do this, you may also be able to do so.

Step 3. Understand that emotional and behavioural problems stem largely from unhealthy beliefs

All approaches to counselling and psychotherapy have their theories about what determines our emotional and behavioural problems. The approach to counselling that I practise holds that what largely determine these problems are the unhealthy beliefs that we hold about important events in our lives. Thus, from my perspective this third step to personal change involves your acknowledging the important role that your beliefs play in determining and perpetuating your psychological problems.

Step 4. Analyse specific examples of your problems and identify the specific unhealthy beliefs that underpin these problems

The fourth step to personal change emphasizes the importance of being as specific as possible at the beginning of the change process. The reason for choosing specific examples of your problems to analyse is that these examples yield reliable information about what you actually felt in specific problem situations, what you did in these situations and, most importantly, what you believed in these situations. There will be ample opportunity for you to generalise later, but at this point of the change process, the more specific you can be the better.

Step 5. Understand what are the healthy alternatives to your unhealthy beliefs

Before you challenge the unhealthy beliefs you hold in problem situations, it is important to appreciate that there are viable healthy alternatives to these beliefs. In all my self-help books, I argue that unhealthy beliefs are rigid and extreme in nature whereas healthy beliefs are intrinsically flexible and non-extreme. It is these latter beliefs that you need to see as realistic alternatives to your unhealthy beliefs.

Step 6. Challenge your unhealthy beliefs and acknowledge that they are false, illogical and unhelpful

The best first step to take in undermining your unhealthy beliefs is to challenge them. Ask yourself whether they are true, sensible in the circumstances and, most importantly, whether they help you or hinder you in your quest for mental health and happiness. In my self-help books I give precise instructions concerning how to do this, and I show why such beliefs are in general false, illogical and largely unproductive.

Step 7. Acknowledge that your healthy beliefs are true, sensible and helpful

It is not sufficient to challenge your unhealthy beliefs: you also have to question the healthy alternatives to these beliefs in the same way. In the vast majority of cases, you will acknowledge that your healthy beliefs are true, sensible and conducive to your mental well-being.

Step 8. Act on your new healthy beliefs

While challenging your unhealthy beliefs cognitively is an important first step to changing them, unless you act in ways that are inconsistent with such beliefs and in ways that are consistent with their healthy alternatives, you will not, in fact, change your unhealthy beliefs. Thus, action is a crucial ingredient in facilitating personal change.

Step 9. Keep challenging your unhealthy beliefs and acting on your healthy beliefs until you disbelieve the former and believe the latter

As I have stressed throughout this talk, the keys to personal change that is not fleeting are effort, repetition and persistence. Thus, it is important for you to challenge your unhealthy beliefs in thought and in deed repeatedly, persistently and with force and energy, and unless you do so, any change in belief will be short lived.

Step 10. Apply the above self-change sequence across the board

You can use the sequence of self-help steps that I have outlined so far not only in situations where you actually experience problems, but also as a general method of facilitating change. Thus, if you have worked on overcoming a specific fear of asserting yourself with your boss, you can then ask yourself who else you are scared of asserting yourself with and apply with them the same steps you took with your boss. In this way you can broaden and extend the gains you have made in tackling specific examples of your problems, and in doing so you will begin to change more general core unhealthy beliefs.

Step 11. Recognise that lapses will occur and accept these when they occur and learn from them

Personal change is rarely linear, and you will experience lapses along the path towards overcoming your problems. It is important that you understand this fact of psychological life and do not disturb yourself about these lapses. If you develop a realistic attitude towards personal change and the hiccups you will experience along the way, you will prevent your lapses from developing into a full-blown relapse. In addition, developing this realistic attitude towards lapses will enable you to stand back and learn from them, so that you get on with the difficult business of tackling your problems armed with increasing knowledge about what factors trigger a lapse and how to deal effectively with them.

Step 12. Identify, in advance, events that you are vulnerable to and use your newly learned self-change methods to confront and deal with them productively

Dealing effectively with lapses involves your learning from them after they have occurred. In addition, you can learn to tackle what I call your vulnerability factors in order to avoid encountering them unprepared. Doing so involves your identifying events which you would disturb yourself about should you face them, spotting the unhealthy beliefs that make these events vulnerability factors for you, and challenging and changing these beliefs in the same way that you challenged and changed the unhealthy beliefs that lay at the core of your original problems. Then, armed with your new healthy beliefs, you should strive to practise them in situations that you find problematic and that you would normally go out of your way to avoid.

A word of caution here. I suggest that you follow a principle that I have called 'challenging, but not overwhelming', which means that you would choose to confront a difficult situation that would constitute a challenge for you, rather than one that would be overwhelming for you at any given point of time. If you follow this principle, after a while you will find very few situations overwhelming, particularly if you strengthen your conviction in your healthy beliefs.

Step 13. Apply self-change methods for the rest of your life

Implementing this final step involves your acknowledging that, if you wish to maintain personal change and extend it across the board, then you will need to apply the self-change methods that you have learned for the rest of your life. This isn't as drastic as it may sound, and will not usually involve much time and effort as long as you have consolidated your healthy beliefs. You will quite readily acknowledge that if you stop caring for yourself physically your health will deteriorate: you would regard as preposterous the idea that you could achieve a level of physical well-being and maintain it no matter how much you subsequently neglected yourself. Therefore, why should you be surprised that you need to take regular steps to maintain and extend your psychological well-being? Taking such steps when you feel fine psychologically may seem strange, but do so and you will increase the chances that you will live a mentally healthier and happier life.

The main limitation of self-help books

All psychological methods have their limits, and even if you take all the steps discussed above, you will still find that there are limits to self-help books. Let me discuss the main limitation of these books in the time that I have available.

The main limitation of self-help books is that they are not written especially for you. In order to help yourself from reading a book, you will have to extrapolate from what the author has written and apply it to your own unique situation. Some people find doing this more easily than others, and if you find such extrapolation and application difficult you may benefit from consulting a counsellor who practises an approach that is consistent with that put forward by the author of the book you are attempting to follow. I find that my self-help books very nicely complement my face-to-face counselling work with clients in that I can help them to apply my general points to their particular circumstances.

I have already mentioned that personal change is not linear and that you will experience obstacles to continued improvement. While good self-help books will alert you to some of the major obstacles to continued progress, they may not cover the very obstacle that may be holding you back. If you think that this may be the case for you, seeking guidance on this issue from a counsellor of the same school as the writer of the self-help book is probably the best way forward. A good self-help book, however, will alert you to this possibility and recommend face-to-face consultation in these circumstances.

Self-help books: for better or worse

I have just mentioned one characteristic of a good self-help book. Let me very briefly set out some of the other characteristics of good examples of this genre and what distinguishes these from self-help books that are less useful.

1. Good self-help books tend to be written by those with professional credentials

While this point does not guarantee that a self-help book will be good, it does at least show you that the author knows what he or she is talking about and is qualified to write with professionally sanctioned authority.

2. Good self-help books tend to be written in clear, jargon-free language

Good self-help books tend to be written in clear everyday language, and, while they do not patronize their readership, they do not assume that this audience has specialised knowledge that they cannot be expected to have.

3. Good self-help books make realistic, not grandiose, claims

Good self-help books, while offering hope that personal change is possible, do not make grandiose claims that you can change your life completely or change your personality. Be especially sceptical of any promotional blurb that promises you the earth. (However, be aware that authors do not always have control over the content of such material, and unscrupulous publishers may not even show the author what some overly enthusiastic publicist has written.)

4. Good self-help books provide concrete steps for you to follow

Many self-help books give very general guidelines about how you can implement a personal change programme, and in my experience many people find it very difficult to follow these general principles on their own. The better self-help books provide very concrete steps that you can follow, but are not dogmatic in claiming that you have to follow these steps slavishly in the order that they appear in the book.

5. Good self-help books make it clear that they are putting forward a perspective, not the perspective

The field of counselling and psychotherapy is not a unified one. This means that there are a number of different perspectives on a given emotional problem. A good self-help book makes it clear which perspective is being taken and stresses that this is one perspective among many. Bad self-help books claim that the author's approach is the only approach to the problem that is worthy of consideration.

6. Good self-help books are based on an approach where there is research evidence

There is a growing body of research on the efficacy of psychological techniques and good self-help books draw upon this body of evidence. This is another reason why it is important that self-help books be written by people who are professionally trained, in that they are familiar with this research evidence, know how to evaluate its quality and are fully aware of its limitations. Authors without this professional background far too often take this research at face value – if, indeed, they are aware of its existence at all.

Incidentally, some people in the field take the radical position that a self-help book should not be published if it has not been shown, by research, to be effective in controlled studies. I think that this restriction is taking things too far, and if applied rigorously would mean that very few self-help books would be published at all and that you, the reading public, would be deprived of much valuable self-help material.

7. Good self-help books recognise the difficulty of personal change
Finally, good self-help books recognise the difficulty of making and sustaining personal change and they repeat this message, as I have done here, throughout.

Conclusion
Let me conclude by reiterating my main message. No matter how good a self-help book is, I want to remind you that *it won't work*. Rather, you will have to make it work by putting into practice repeatedly the clear, step-by-step guidelines to personal change that hopefully the author has provided.

Remember that change is difficult, uncomfortable, time-consuming and involves sustained effort. If you follow this principle and still make no progress, it is useful to consult a counsellor to discuss what may be going wrong; or it may be that the approach outlined in the self-help book that you are following is not the right one for you.

While I might have been expected to end my talk on an upbeat note of enthusiastic optimism – after all, I would like you all to buy my new book, which by the way is called *Overcoming Shame* (Dryden, 1997) – it is no bad thing to end on a note of realism. So, buy my book and realise that it won't work. However, if you are prepared to commit yourself to working hard to overcoming your life-inhibiting feelings of shame, and recognise that doing so requires sustained effort, is time-consuming and involves discomfort, then the combination of your realistic view about personal change and my realistic views on how to tackle shame should bear fruit.

References
Dryden, W. (1994). *Ten steps to positive living*. London: Sheldon Press.
Dryden, W. (1997). *Overcoming shame*. London: Sheldon Press.

11

rationality, outrageous ideas and sensitivity

In my opinion this is one of the most controversial lectures that I have ever delivered. It was given as a Keynote Address on May 31, 1997 at the 1st International Conference on Counselling Psychology organised by the Division of Counselling Psychology of the British Psychological Society which took place at Stratford-upon-Avon. Nobody walked out of the talk and the discussion after the lecture was strangely muted. Either I overestimated the controversial nature of the lecture or the audience was dumbstruck!

In this talk, I am going to present some ideas that are derived from the theory of Rational Emotive Behaviour Therapy. If presented without explanation, these ideas will seem outrageous, but when embedded in the context of REBT theory they make perfect sense. I suppose at the outset I should issue a health warning, in that you may find some of what I say shocking and even offensive. You may even feel tempted to walk out. This is, of course, your prerogative. However, I would much prefer you to stay, express your displeasure and argue with me, so that we can have a dialogue about what I have presented.

While much has been written about desirable counsellor qualities and attitudes, little has been written about the ability of counsellors to hear all manner of things from clients without being shocked by what they hear. My view is that the unshockability of counsellors is a much under-rated therapeutic condition. If the counsellor conveys that she (in this case) will not be shocked by what the client says, then she will create a space where the client will dare to speak the unspeakable and think the unthinkable. In this spirit, I will say things that you thought you would never hear in a keynote address at a distinguished gathering. Allow me, for a brief period, to mention the unmentionable.

Beyond belief: the shocking ABCs of REBT
One of the core theoretical ideas of REBT is represented by the ABC model of human emotions. This can be summed up neatly by the statement: 'People are disturbed [at C] not by things [at A], but by their rigid and extreme views of things [at B].' For Albert Ellis, the founder of REBT, these rigid and extreme beliefs are at the very core of much psychological disturbance. As is now well known in the field of counselling and psychotherapy, dogmatic beliefs come in the form of 'musts', absolutistic 'shoulds', 'have-to's, etc., and are the breeding ground for three other irrational beliefs which are extreme in nature. These are known as: awfulising beliefs, low frustration tolerance beliefs, and beliefs where self, others and life conditions are deprecated.

The healthy alternative to these four irrational beliefs are essentially flexible and non-extreme in nature. These rational or healthy beliefs are known as preferences, anti-awfulising beliefs, high frustration tolerance beliefs and beliefs where self, others and life conditions are accepted.

Now the ABC model of REBT is not controversial until you begin to consider events at A which are highly aversive. Let's take rape, for example. The ABC model of REBT states as follows: women (in this case) are disturbed not by being raped, but by their rigid and extreme views of being raped. Now, I can well appreciate that for some of you this is a monstrous statement. A woman has been raped and now I (a man no less) am saying that this event did not cause her disturbed feelings, but that she made herself disturbed by holding a set of rigid and extreme beliefs about being raped. How insensitive and how inaccurate. Furthermore, you may think that I am blaming the victim and minimising the responsibility of the man committing the rape. I can understand if this is your reaction; for, stated in this stark manner, the idea that a woman causes her own disturbed feelings about being raped is insensitive and I would never put this in such a stark way to clients.

Imagine this scene. A woman has been raped and seeks counselling. She is sobbing uncontrollably, at which point the counsellor tries to show her that she is making herself disturbed about being raped. Is this insensitive? Of course it is, and no good REBT therapist would intervene in this way. A sensitive and empathic response is called for, and this is what the REBT therapist would offer. And yet, no matter how empathic and sensitive the counsellor is, this does not change the fact that the client *is* disturbing herself by the beliefs that she holds about the rape. But she is light years away from being able to hear this perspective. She is, however, closer to hearing that being raped can be said to be causing her distress.

REBT makes a crucial distinction between healthy negative emotions (or *distress*) and unhealthy negative emotions (or *disturbance*). Distress stems from rational beliefs and disturbance stems from irrational beliefs. Ruling out very unlikely reactions to rape such as pleasure and indifference, one can feel either distressed or disturbed about being raped. Now, given that irrational beliefs are dogmatic and extreme versions of rational beliefs, one can argue that it is highly likely that virtually everyone who is raped has a set of healthy beliefs about this very aversive activating event.

Thus, the woman in question is likely to have a very strong preference not to be raped, views it as something very, very bad and so on. These beliefs are so ubiquitous that we can say that being raped causes distress, whether this distress is overt or covert. But since irrational beliefs are rigid and extreme versions of these rational beliefs, they are not caused by the event (although I note in passing that the more aversive the rape, the more likely it is that the person will transform her rational beliefs into irrational beliefs); no, these rigid and extreme transformations of rational beliefs are the responsibility of the person who is raped.

This does not mean, of course, that we should blame the woman for her disturbance. It means that we are empowering her. I'll say that again. Helping the woman at a therapeutically sensitive time to acknowledge that she is responsible for her disturbance is an act of empowerment. It is empowering because it enables the client to free herself from her disturbed feelings. She may not get over her healthy distress (although this will probably lessen over time), nor should we want her to, for it is healthy for her to be distressed about such a highly aversive activating event as rape. But she does not have to be disturbed for an unduly long period about this event. She has the ability to transcend this experience in a healthy manner, and it is this realisation that is empowering.

She can accomplish this, according to REBT theory, by doing two things. First, she can rid herself of the rigid and extreme versions of her rational beliefs. Examples of such extreme versions are 'Being raped makes me a dirty, repulsive person' and 'My life is completely ruined.' Second, she can actively stay with the flexible, non-extreme beliefs that are at the core of her healthy distress (e.g. 'Being raped is a disgusting thing to have happened to me, but it does not define me as a person. I am not a dirty person: I am a person to whom a dirty thing was done' and 'My life has been badly affected, but not completely ruined. "Ruined" means that I cannot recover, but I can recover even though I may never forget it and may be somewhat influenced by it.'

Let me stress that it is probably normal for women (and men) who have been raped to be disturbed about it, but normal does not mean healthy. If we want to help people to overcome their disturbance, but not their distress, we can help them to remove what they themselves have added, i.e. the rigid and extreme beliefs which are not an intrinsic part of the rape. This needs to be done with great sensitivity at a time when the client is ready to benefit from it, and it should be emphasized that the client should not be blamed for needlessly, but understandably, adding irrational beliefs to the experience.

Finally, this work can be done without minimising either the aversiveness of the rape or the responsibility of the person who perpetrated the rape. Let me be perfectly clear about this. Rape is an act of violence and the person perpetrating the rape is to be held fully responsible for it. The position that I have taken with respect to the source of disturbance does not detract one iota from this point.

Taking offense at 'shoulds'

In REBT, as in life, the meaning of words is important. Unless I am clear about the meaning of a word that I am using, you may easily take offence at what I say and may even think that I am crazy for saying it.

Let me take the word 'should', for example. As I have already mentioned, REBT theory posits that rigid beliefs are at the core of much psychological disturbance. Such beliefs take the form of 'musts', 'got to's and 'have to's. They also take the form of 'shoulds', but only when these shoulds are absolute. The word 'should' has several different meanings in the English language, and this fact can lead to confusion at best, and to your taking offence and even my incarceration in a psychiatric hospital at worst.

Listen carefully to my next statement and note your immediate reaction to it. 'The Holocaust should have happened.' Have you taken offense at that statement? Are you angry at me for saying it? Do you think that I have taken leave of my senses or think that I am a member of the British National Party? I am neither mad nor a Nazi. All I have done is to use the word 'should' in a manner to convey one meaning, and you have reacted as if I have used the word 'should' in a way that conveys a very different meaning.

It follows therefore that when using language in REBT (or in any other approach to counselling) it is very important first, to be aware that a single word has different meanings and second, to take great care in differentiating and explaining these meanings when using these words with clients. This is precisely what I deliberately did not do when stating without any explanation that the holocaust should have happened. I mentioned earlier that timing of one's interventions is a mark of therapeutic sensitivity. Here I am arguing that the explanation of terms that might be otherwise misinterpreted without further elaboration is another hallmark of such sensitivity.

Let me now consider the different meanings of the word 'should' before returning to my statement about the Holocaust. The first meaning of the word 'should' that I want to consider is the absolute should. This is the only 'should' that represents an irrational belief. An example of an irrational, absolute should is as follows: 'You should not have treated me in this way.' What the person really means here is: 'You absolutely should not have treated me in this way.' In this example, the person is demanding or insisting that the other person not act in a certain way towards him. An irrational, absolute 'should' also leads the person to hold one or more further irrational beliefs which Ellis (1994) views as being derivatives from this absolute 'should' (e.g. 'It's terrible that you treated me in this way', 'I can't stand the fact that you treated me in this way' and 'You are a swine for treating me in this way'). The absolute 'should' also leads to an unhealthy negative emotion, and in this example the person experienced demanding, condemnatory anger towards the other who treated him badly. As I mentioned earlier, the absolute 'should' is the only 'should' that represents an irrational belief and is thus the only 'should' that is the target for change in REBT.

The second 'should' that I wish to discuss is the preferential 'should'. This is the healthy alternative to the absolute 'should' and contains an implicit negation of it. If we make both the preferential nature of this 'should' and this negation explicit in our example, we get the following statement: 'You preferably should not have treated me in this way, but there is no law that states that you absolutely should not have done so.' As you can just hear this sounds very awkward, so the person is more likely to say: 'You should not have treated me in this way.' This is, of course, confusing, since it is exactly the same wording as was used to denote an absolute 'should'. However, a preferential 'should' leads to different effects from the absolute 'should'. First, it leads to a further set of rational beliefs (e.g. 'It's bad that you treated me in this way, but it is not terrible', 'It's difficult, but I can stand the fact that you treated me in this way', and 'You are not a swine for treating me in this way, but an unrateable fallible human being who has acted badly'). The preferential 'should' also leads to a healthy negative emotion, and in this example the person experienced non-demanding, non-condemnatory anger about the other person's mistreatment of him. As the preferential 'should' is healthy, it is not targeted for change in REBT.

The third type of 'should' is the recommendatory 'should'. Here, for example, you may recommend that a person take a particular course of action as in the statement: 'You should you put your money into a PEP.' Assuming that the person is acting in good faith, what she is saying here is that she thinks that it would be good for you to take out a PEP and this is what she recommends you to do. While the content of the recommendation may be questioned an REBT therapist would not question the recommendatory 'should' since it is not, by itself, dogmatic.

The fourth 'should' that exists is the predictive should. When you use the term 'should' in this way, you are predicting what will happen based on past experience. An example of this type of 'should' is found in the statement: 'The 6.05 from Waterloo should be five minutes late, since it usually is.' This type of 'should' is again not usually targeted for change in REBT.

The fifth 'should' that I wish to consider is the conditional 'should'. Here the person specifies the conditions that have to be met for an outcome to be achieved (e.g. 'If I study hard, I should pass my exams'). There is, of course, an element of prediction about this 'should', but its defining characteristic is in the specification of the conditions that have to be met for something else to occur. Conditional 'shoulds' frequently point to occurrences in the future, hence the overlap with predictive 'shoulds'. However, neither this 'should' nor the next is questioned in REBT since neither is implicated in psychological disturbance.

A sixth 'should' that exists is the ideal 'should'. This is really a special sub-type of the conditional 'should' and is more formally known as the ideal conditional 'should' in that it specifies a relationship between the meeting of ideal conditions and a particular outcome. 'The grey mare should win this race' is an example of the ideal 'should' in that the person is saying that, if ideal conditions exist, the grey mare should (or will) win the race.

A seventh 'should' is one that may be called the deserving 'should'. Here a person is specifying what 'should' occur on the basis of a sense of justice or fairness. 'He should be imprisoned for five years for what he did' is specifying a relationship between what the person did and what 'should' happen if justice is to prevail. It goes without saying that this sense of justice is subjective and will vary from person to person. 'He should get five years for what he did'. 'No, I think he should be hanged for it' is an exchange between two people indicating two different ideas of justice. Deserving 'should's are not targeted for change in REBT unless they are transformed into absolute 'shoulds'.

The eighth and final form of 'should' that I wish to consider is called the empirical 'should'. When the empirical 'should' is used, the person is indicating that she acknowledges that all the conditions were in place for what happened to have happened. Thus, when I use an empirical 'should' in the statement 'The Conservative Party should have lost the election', all I am saying is that all the conditions were in place for them to lose the election – nothing more, nothing less. I am not indicating my personal preference in this statement, nor I am appealing to any sense of deservingness. I am outlining what happened and stating that it should have happened because it did; i.e., all the conditions existed for it to happen. As such, the empirical 'should' is not the target for change in REBT.

Let me now return to my statement: 'The Holocaust should have happened.' In this statement, I am not saying that this is what I wanted to happen, nor am I saying that this was my recommendation. Furthermore, I am not saying that the Jews deserved their fate, nor am I saying that this is what ideally should have happened. All I am saying is that all the conditions were in place for it to happen – nothing more, nothing less. But, because my statement could have several different meanings, you can be forgiven if you thought that I was saying something very different. Because of this confusion over the meaning of the word 'should', I suggest that whenever possible we qualify the word when we use it and explain exactly what we mean. Thus, in my original statement what I meant was this: Tragically, catastrophically, unforgettably and shockingly, all the conditions were in place nearly sixty years ago for the Holocaust to have occurred, and thus, the Holocaust should have happened because tragically, catastrophically, unforgettably and shockingly, it did.

On thinking the unthinkable
As I have stressed several times, rigid beliefs can be expressed as 'musts', absolute 'shoulds', 'got to's and 'have to's. However they are expressed, they have many deleterious effects. REBT theory has focused a lot of attention on the impact of holding rigid beliefs on the way we feel and act. But it has also, more recently, studied the effects of holding these beliefs on the way that we think. I have referred to these latter effects as the *cognitive consequences* of holding dogmatic 'musts' and absolute 'shoulds'. Thus, with Frank Bond and others, I have discovered that if

you hold a dogmatic demand you are much more likely subsequently to make a range of negatively distorted inferences than if you hold a flexible, healthy preference (Bond & Dryden, 1996).

If you hold a dogmatic demand, you are also more likely to develop a pattern of obsessive thinking, if you are so prone, than if you hold a non-dogmatic preference. Let me illustrate this with an actual case which I relate to you with the client's permission, as there is hardly any chance that the person can be identified from what I will tell you now. The two therapeutic factors that I wish to highlight here are counsellor unshockability and the importance of explaining to clients how they unwittingly help to create and elaborate their own obsessions. Without the presence of the former, clients will not disclose the true nature of their obsessions. Without the latter, they will remain scared that they will completely lose control of themselves, a fear that will prevent them from healthily resolving this problem.

This client, who I will call Sally, was a regular churchgoer. She had little sexual education and was a virgin. One day when she was in church her mind wandered and she found herself looking at a statue of Christ and in particular, gazing at Christ's nipples. She was horrified about this, primarily because she held the belief that while she was in church her thoughts had to be thoroughly pure. Given this demand, she tried not to look at the statue, but, typically in such cases, she began to have involuntary unwanted thoughts about the naked Jesus and started to look at Christ's crotch. She redoubled her efforts not to think about and look at Christ in this way, forbidding herself to do so in an absolute fashion. She also went to different churches, hoping that she could leave behind her growing obsession. She could not. At her latest church she began to have fantasies about having sex with Christ, and with every redoubled attempt to banish these thoughts and fantasies, they increased both in number and in vividness of sexual content. When I first saw her, it transpired – for it took her many weeks for her to tell me this – that she had begun to think about having oral sex with Christ while being taken from behind by the local vicar.

Using REBT theory, I helped this woman to understand how her thoughts and images had developed from innocently gazing at Christ's nipples to a scene more at home in the steamy world of explicit adult videos. Her task was to go back to church and to allow herself to think and imagine anything that she thought and imagined. She was to banish nothing from her mind. Of course, I told her it was healthy for her to be strongly desirous of not thinking and imagining such distasteful things, but there was no earthly (or heavenly) reason why she must be free of such cognitive phenomena. I also helped her to see the difference between having so-called shameful thoughts and being a shameful person. In short, I helped her to accept herself as a fallible human being who was not immune from thinking inappropriate and shocking things. It will come as no surprise to you that this woman believed that she always had to say and do the right thing as well as to think the right thoughts. She was a walking example of dogmatic moral correctness. Later in counselling I helped her to join the human race on this issue and surrender her wings.

Parenthetically, after the establishment of a working alliance, the judicious use of humour is particularly therapeutic in such cases. At the end of counselling Sally was back at her old church virtually free of her troubling thoughts. When she gets them she reminds herself of something that I want to leave you with: that sometimes it is therapeutic to go to church and think about giving Christ a blow job while being taken from behind by the local vicar.

Oedipus schmoedipus : why you don't have to gouge your eyes out when you have discovered that you have killed your father and married your mother
Most of you will be familiar with the story of Oedipus. For those of you who are not, let me briefly relate this tragic tale. The *Chambers Biographical Dictionary* (Magnusson, 1990: 1098) states that Oedipus was the

> '. . . *Greek legendary figure, who killed his father, Laius, and married his mother, Jocasta . . . An oracle had warned Laius, king of Thebes, that he would be killed by his son. Laius therefore exposed the infant Oedipus to die on the mountains after piercing his feet with a spike (hence the name Oedipus, which in Greek means 'with swollen feet'). The young Oedipus was rescued and adopted by Polybus, king of Corinth, and grew up with the belief that the rulers of Corinth were his parents. When told by an oracle that he was fated to kill his father and marry his mother, he left Corinth in an attempt to avoid fulfilling the prophecy. On his way through Boeotia, he was involved in a quarrel with his (to him unknown) father Laius, and killed him. He freed Thebes from the scourge of the Sphinx by solving her riddles, and in return married the now-widowed Jocasta, his mother, and became king of Thebes. At length, the terrible truth about his origins and parenthood was revealed to him. Jocasta took her life and Oedipus blinded himself.'*

As you all know, this tale inspired Sigmund Freud, who coined the term 'Oedipus complex' to describe a young boy's longing to oust his father and have his mother for himself. I want to focus on a different part of the story and argue that Oedipus's act of self-blinding stemmed from an irrational belief. I am going to show you that there was no need for Oedipus to gouge his eyes out and no need for him to feel guilty about what he did.

Let's assume that I was alive at the time and practising REBT and that Oedipus, in an obvious state of disturbance, consulted me. This is how I would have endeavoured to help him.

Windy: OK, Oedipus, what's your problem?

Oedipus: I'm in a terrible state. I have committed two terrible sins.

Windy: What are they?

Oedipus: I've killed my father and married and slept with my mother?

Windy: Did you know that they were your mother and father before you killed the former and married the latter?

Oedipus: No, but that doesn't help me. People have tried to comfort me by reminding me that I didn't know this, but I still want to gouge my eyes out.

Windy: OK, which crime shall we discuss first?

Oedipus: Let's start with the murder of my father, Laius.

Windy: OK, how do you feel about killing your father?

Oedipus: Very guilty.

Windy: Right. Let me put this into REBT's ABC framework. A, which stands for the activating event, is murdering your father, and C, which stands for your emotional consequence, is guilt.

Oedipus: What's B?

Windy: B stands for the beliefs that you hold about murdering your father which account for your guilt. In REBT, A (i.e. in this case your murdering your father), does not cause C, (i.e. your guilt): B does.

Oedipus: So what are my beliefs?

Windy: Well, let me put forward a couple of hunches and you correct me if I'm wrong. First, I think you are demanding that you absolutely should not have killed your father and second, I think that you believe that you are a thoroughly rotten person for killing him. Am I right?

Oedipus: That's exactly right. But aren't I a rotten person for killing my father?

Windy: Of course not. Let's leave aside for a moment that you didn't know that he was your father and accept that you did a rotten thing. How are you a rotten person for doing this rotten thing?

Oedipus: Well, I killed my father.

Windy: I'm not disputing that. Killing your father was wrong, it was a rotten deed, but how are you rotten through and through for doing this rotten thing?

Oedipus:	I guess I'm not.
Windy:	Why not?
Oedipus:	Because as you say, one rotten deed does not make me rotten through and through.
Windy:	That's right. If you were rotten through and through, you could never do anything good, but we know that you freed Thebes from the scourge of the Sphinx. Wasn't that a good deed
Oedipus:	Yes it was.
Windy:	But if you were a rotten person how could you have done such a noble deed?
Oedipus:	You're right, I couldn't.
Windy:	So if you aren't a rotten person, what are you?
Oedipus:	I'm a fallible human being who can't be rated by my actions. Being fallible means that I can do good deed and bad deeds.
Windy:	That's exactly right. Now, it's healthy to feel badly about your bad deeds, and consequently it would be healthy if you were to feel very remorseful about killing your father. But guilt is an unhealthy emotion which could lead you to blind yourself. Is that clear?
Oedipus:	So remorse is healthy and guilt isn't.
Windy:	That's right, remorse stems from your rational belief and guilt from your irrational belief. Now let's look at the other part of your belief: 'I absolutely shouldn't have killed my father.' Where is the law of the universe that states that you absolutely should not have done that?
Oedipus:	Well it was very, very wrong.
Windy:	You'll get no argument from me on that score, but being human are you immune from doing very, very, bad acts?
Oedipus:	No, I don't have that immunity. But I was warned that I would kill my father. I absolutely should have known what I was doing and refrained from doing it.
Windy:	Well, that would have been highly desirable, but does it follow that because it would have been highly desirable that you knew it was your father, therefore you absolutely should have known? Are you an oracle in your spare time?
Oedipus:	Point taken.
Windy:	And incidentally, if there was a law of the universe forbidding you from killing your father, there's no way that you could have killed him because you would have had to follow that law.
Oedipus:	Right, reality should be reality however tragic it is.
Windy:	Well put. Now I suggest that you go over these ideas for

	homework and next week I'll help you to get over your disturbed feelings about marrying your mother.
Oedipus:	And also can we deal with my feelings of shame when others view me as an object of disgust?
Windy:	We can indeed.
Oedipus:	Great. How much do I owe you?
Windy:	£85.
Oedipus:	That's a small price to pay for saving my eyesight.
Windy:	See you and be seen by you next week.

I wish to stress two points from this interchange. First, it is important that I agree with Oedipus that his 'crimes' were heinous. It is fundamental to REBT strategy that I do not try to show him what he already acknowledged, albeit intellectually: that he neither knew his father before he killed him nor knew his mother before he married her. Oedipus will be more open to this type of intervention once he has made strides in accepting himself for his 'crimes'. Second, it is important to distinguish between normal, understandable responses on the one hand and healthy responses on the other. While it is very understandable and statistically normal for Oedipus to condemn himself for his actions, this does not mean that it is healthy for him to do so. If I do not target for change his guilt-producing, self-condemnatory belief, he will remain vulnerable to deliberate self-harm.

Conclusion
In summary, I have discussed why being raped does not disturb you, why the Holocaust should have happened, why it is sometimes therapeutic to think about giving Christ a blow job while being taken from behind by the local vicar, and why it is not necessary to gouge your eyes out after killing your father and marrying your mother.

Before I close, let me provide you with an alternative summary. I have discussed the empowering nature of the ABCs of REBT, but stressed that this framework has to be used with great sensitivity, particularly when clients' activating events are very aversive. I have considered eight different meanings of the word 'should' and stressed the intended therapeutic benefits of differentiating these meanings to avoid the serious problems that can arise from misunderstanding the meaning of the word. I then argued that, when working with clients with obsessive thinking, it is beneficial to explain how thoughts spiral out of our control in direct proportion to our dogmatic attempts to control them and to stress the therapeutic benefits of thinking the unthinkable. Finally, I have discussed the unhealthiness of guilt and shown how to intervene to prevent its sometimes tragic consequences.

Rational Emotive Behaviour Therapy is based on a set of ideas that can be both enlightening and outrageous. I have reviewed some of these ideas and promise to review more in a future volume tentatively titled: *Strange, but Rational.*

References

Bond, F.W., & Dryden, W. (1996). Modifying irrational control and certainty beliefs: clinical recommendations based upon research. In W. Dryden (ed.), *Research in counselling and psychotherapy: practical applications.* London: Sage.

Magnusson, M. (ed.) (1990). *Chambers biographical dictionary.* Edinburgh: Chambers.

12

looking for the good
in Hitler
and acknowledging the bad
in Mother Teresa

This lecture was the 74th in the Public Lecture Series of the Associates of the University Counselling Service at the University of East Anglia on December 12, 1997. It was especially significant for me since it was the last in this long-running lecture series to be presided over by Professor Brian Thorne who was retiring from full-time service at the University that month. Brian continues to work part-time at UEA, running the University's Diploma in Counselling programme with Judy Moore. In effect, the change means that Brian has two full-time jobs rather than three!

Brian is perhaps the most reliable, conscientious and supportive person that I have encountered in the field of counselling. I value my professional relationship with Brian enormously and I was pleased to be a part of this occasion. Brian is no stranger to controversy himself, so I knew that I had at least one kindred spirit in the audience for another of my controversial lectures. As it transpired, the lecture was very well received and led to a lively but reflective discussion.

In this talk, I will argue that flexibility is central to our well-being and development as human beings and that this quality is germane to effective counselling. I will explore the implications of this view, some of which you may very well find shocking. If so, blame Brian Thorne since he invited me to speak this evening!

Twelve men attempt to merge with or break through a wall

Let me begin by taking you back to an all-heterosexual male sexuality group that I attended almost twenty years ago. What was unique about this structured group experience was that it was facilitated by a woman. One of the exercises that she asked us to do was to imagine a line running between the left-hand and the right-hand walls of the room that we were in. We were asked to think of the left-hand wall as indicating 100% heterosexuality and the right-hand wall as indicating 100% homosexuality and to place ourselves along this line so as to represent our views of our own sexual orientation. The ensuing scene was a sight to behold as a group of grown men fought with one another to hug or, in some cases, to break through a brick wall! I don't think you need to ask which wall we all tried to merge with or smash down.

Once we had calmed down enough to process our reactions to this exercise, we began to understand our responses. We were terrified of admitting to ourselves and to others in the group that we had experienced any thoughts, feelings or reactions that could in any way be seen as homosexual. Now, it is not possible for any man, let alone a group of a dozen men, to claim with any authority that he has never had such a thought, feeling or reaction. Once we began to accept ourselves and the others in the group as complex human beings, we could admit to having a sexuality that defied black or white categories.

The creation and maintenance of obsessive, unwanted thoughts

This dogmatic attitude about sexuality can have decided disturbed effects. Thus, I once counselled a man who had developed an obsession about being homosexual even though there was little in his history to indicate that he was gay. His obsession was rooted in a pornographic video that he had seen which had a scene depicting oral sex between men. A few days later he dreamt about this event, but without any accompanying feelings of desire. However, he was so horrified by the fact that he had had this dream that he became convinced that he was homosexual, which if true meant that he would have to kill himself, so devastating would this be for his view of himself. This man held a belief that he must not, under any circumstances, have a single thought that was homosexual in content. As you can imagine, this led to an increase of such thoughts, and as they increased he redoubled his desperate attempts to exclude them from his consciousness. These redoubled desperate attempts only served to amplify the vividness and explicitness of his thoughts in this domain.

As most of you know, I am a practitioner of Rational Emotive Behaviour Therapy, an approach to counselling that places a high value on flexibility. The traditional REBT initial approach to this man would be to ask him to assume temporarily that he *was* homosexual and to encourage him to accept himself for this. I suspected that this would not work with him and I was soon proved right. He became very agitated when I took this line because in his disturbed frame of mind he thought I was telling him that *I* thought he was homosexual.

Since I am not a dogmatic practitioner of REBT, I changed tack and was much more successful at showing him two things. First, I helped him to see that his desperate insistence that he experience only heterosexual thoughts, and his belief that he must never think anything that could vaguely be construed as homosexual, in fact increased the likelihood that he *would* think such unwanted thoughts and that they would increase in number and become more explicit, the more desperately he tried *not* to have them. Second, I showed him that he was seeing only two options: either he was heterosexual (which meant to him having no homosexual thoughts), or he was homosexual. I helped him to see that people can be placed along a continuum and that it was entirely possible, and in his terminology 'normal', to be heterosexual and to have the occasional homosexual thought. I also related to him the wall incident in the male sexuality group that I told you about earlier. My client accepted this position and practised both of these ideas: that he was straight even though he had the occasional homosexual thought, and that the reason he was flooded by these thoughts now was due to his misguided attempt to be absolutely free of them. With this more flexible philosophy, he calmed down and stopped being obsessed with his thoughts and with his sexual orientation.

So the message is this: if you try to exclude various unwanted thoughts from your awareness, and in particular if you do so in a dogmatic way, you will increase the number, frequency, explicit content and vividness of these thoughts and you will disturb yourself about their presence. However, if you recognise that as a person you are not immune from unwanted thoughts and you allow yourself to have them, then these thoughts will decrease in number, frequency, explicit content and vividness and you will be healthily concerned and disappointed rather than unhealthily anxious and ashamed about their presence.

Attempting to be totally different from your parents
This dogmatic attempt to exclude an experience can often relate to clients' views of their childhood. Thus, a man recently consulted me for an anxiety problem that he had about money. It transpired that money

was a core conflictual area between his parents when he was growing up, both of whom were in the client's words 'hopeless about money'. Until recently, my client had always managed his finances well, and it was when this management began to break down that his anxiety started, which by the time that I first saw him had increased to the level of panic. At the root of this man's anxiety was a rigid belief that he must be nothing like his parents when it came to money and that his recent financial difficulties meant to him that he was just like them, an inference that was accompanied with much self-hate.

This man's distorted inference that 'I am just like my parents when it comes to money' was created by his dogmatic insistence that he must not be anything like them on this issue. I helped my client by encouraging him to see that, while it may be advantageous to be nothing like his parents when it came to money, it was very unlikely that he would achieve such immunity for two reasons. First, he was human, and all humans have the potential to mismanage their finances at times. Second, he was biologically and socially influenced by his parents, and it would be strange indeed if he was *nothing* like them on any issue. At the same time, I helped him to distinguish between his current, transitory difficulties with money, which he could healthily dislike, and his entire self, which he could healthily accept. These two strategies helped him to see and fully acknowledge that, while he was having difficulties with money currently, he was far more dissimilar to his parents on this issue than he was similar.

Once we insist that we are nothing like our parents (for example), we put ourselves in a different category from them. In our attempts to ban ourselves from having certain experiences, we become hypervigilant to their possible presence and thus are more likely to detect them. Once we have detected even slight evidence of the experience we are desperately trying to exclude, we disturb ourselves about its presence and grossly exaggerate the threat posed by its presence. In such a frame of mind, we will be unable to stand back and understand what is going on, and thus we will be unable to deal with it.

By contrast, if we accept ourselves as human beings who have the potential to experience anything that human beings are capable of experiencing then we will not place ourselves in a different category from our parents. We will therefore be far less likely to disturb ourselves about the presence of the unwanted experience and will not become hypervigilant to its possible presence. If we do detect slight evidence of the experience, we will be accurate in our judgement that it is slight and we will strive to understand what is going on so that we can deal with it.

Fear of losing self-control

These dynamics are in operation when we consider other areas of disturbed and healthy human functioning. Let me consider, for example, cases where we are scared of losing control of ourselves. When this happens, typically we are demanding that we must always be in control of our feelings and other psychological processes. In these circumstances, when we become aware that our rigid control is beginning to break down we tend to think that this will have dire results. For example, we may think that we will go mad or run amok. Consequently, we try desperately to avoid situations where we think that we may lose self-control. As you may appreciate, this strategy is doomed to failure because there is no guarantee that there is any place that will provide us with the certainty that we will remain in total control of ourselves. You may recognise this dynamic as a core component of the agoraphobic experience.

What can we do in these circumstances? The main thing is to appreciate that dogmatic attempts to remain in control of ourselves are precisely the problem. Paradoxically, the best way to regain control of ourselves is to allow ourselves to experience feeling out of control and to recognise that as humans we are not built to be exempt from such experiences. It is ironic that the role model for people who demand perfect control is not a human being: rather, it is a programmable computer. While computers are not yet capable of experiencing anxiety and anger, two emotions that people with control problems are particularly scared of, this is not true of human beings. Again, it is the rigid belief that we must be in control that leads us to primitive all-or-nothing thinking: either I am in control or I am out of control. In reality, however, as humans we cannot realistically cram our experiences into an 'in control' box or an 'out of control' box . Our experiences are far too rich and fluid for such simple categorisation. Rather, control is best seen as lying along a continuum, the two ends of which are rarely experienced for long periods of time.

It is also a feature of people who have a rigid attitude towards self-control that they regard themselves as weak and defective if they do, in fact, experience some loss of control. These people also think that others will see them as weak and defective if they show publicly that they are losing control of themselves in any way. Interestingly, such people are quite ready to acknowledge that other people are allowed to experience lapses in self-control. But *they* are not allowed – or, more accurately, they do not allow themselves – to experience such lapses. They believe that *they* have to be in total control, and if they are in any way out of control this proves that they are weak and defective, and others will look down on them and scorn them. It is little wonder that shame is the constant emotional companion of people who have an inflexible attitude towards self-control; this emotion lurks in the shadows waiting to be experienced when the person reveals to himself and to others a breakdown in rigid self-control.

The key to helping people with control-related problems involves encouraging them to join the human race and to give up their self-imposed immunity from loss of self-control. Once they can give up the need to be godlike, they can come to earth and, in embracing their uniqueness and their humanity, can lose their fear of their own internal experiences. It is for this reason that their therapists need to embrace their own uniqueness and humanity if they are to be truly helpful to such clients.

On being dogmatically against dogmatism

I want to dwell on this point for a moment, for I have detected a worrying tendency in the field for counsellors to regard their clients as different from themselves. As an example, there is a real danger that Rational Emotive Behaviour Therapists will use REBT theory tyrannically against themselves. For example, this theory clearly distinguishes between healthy and unhealthy negative emotions and holds that flexible beliefs underpin the former and dogmatic beliefs the latter. Clients are encouraged to experience healthy negative emotions such as sadness, remorse and concern when they face aversive activating events instead of experiencing unhealthy negative emotions such as depression, guilt and anxiety.

It is a real temptation for REBT therapists to deny to themselves and to other REBT therapists that they experience unhealthy negative emotions in their own lives. Such counsellors believe that as REBT therapists they are not supposed to disturb themselves by holding dogmatic beliefs about the aversive events that they encounter. In holding such a dogmatic belief – which comically and ironically can be summed up in the phrase 'I must not be dogmatic' – such REBT therapists are, in fact, placing themselves in a different category from their clients and from other people. This shows that human beings have the capacity to take any good idea or philosophy and turn this idea or philosophy into a rigid dogma. Thus, Christians can become dogmatic religionists, humanists can become rigid upholders of non-belief and REBT therapists can adopt a dogmatic stance against their own and other people's dogmas.

Couple conflict and splitting

Dogmatism is the root of many ills in our society and is at the core of the "I am right, you are wrong" idea that permeates our society. This is another instance of primitive black or white thinking which shows up in many forms of interpersonal conflict, of which marital conflict is but one vivid example.

It can be very difficult for some people to admit to themselves and to their partners that they may be largely wrong on a particular issue and that their partners may be largely right. There may be various reasons for this phenomenon. First, one or both partners may believe that they must not be wrong, a rigid view which leads them to locate wrongness in the other person and to defend their own position with rigid relish. Second, the person may think that if he (in this case), admits that he may be wrong then this is an admission of a weakness and may be used against him by his partner. Third, one or both partners may lack a relative view of human endeavours and fail to recognise that in most forms of conflict there are likely to be rights *and* wrongs on both sides and that there are different perspectives to be taken of the same event. Imagine what it would be like if both partners held the following views:

i. In any disagreement with my partner I may be wrong in certain respects. This proves that I am a fallible human being who can be right and wrong, and it is not terrible to admit my errors either to myself or to my partner.

ii. Acknowledging to my partner that I may be wrong is not an admission of weakness. Quite the contrary, it is an admission of strength because I can admit without shame to my essential nature as a human being, which is fallibility.

iii. I hold the same view of my partner as I do of myself on this point.

iv. There is not one way of viewing a disagreement, and it is unlikely that I am completely right and my partner completely wrong on any issue or vice versa. Rather, there are different ways of looking at a topic and I need to understand where my partner is coming from on any issue.

v. It would be nice if my partner held the above beliefs, but she doesn't have to.

It is my opinion that the five attitudes that I have just articulated encourage couple empathy and that partners need to be helped to develop these attitudes before they are taught any communication skills.

Another form of black and white thinking that is found in disturbed couple functioning is splitting. Here, one partner locates 100 per cent of a given quality in himself and 0 per cent in the other person or, of course, vice versa. For example, Jenny sought help from me for agoraphobia. Her husband, James, was very suspicious of therapy and denigrated it as a get-rich-quick panacea for therapists. It transpired that James saw Jenny as a weak woman who needed to be looked after by him. His way of looking after her was to do everything for her outside of the home. He shopped for her and the family, took the children to school and picked them up at the end of the day. Everybody who knew James considered him to be a wonderful husband, as did Jenny herself. However, James put every obstacle imaginable in the way of Jenny's progress in therapy. For example, after agreeing to look after the children to enable Jenny to go out on her own for a short period, he would invariably contrive to cancel this arrangement for 'important work-related' reasons. Also, if he ever took Jenny out so that she could practise gradually acclimatising herself to an unfamiliar environment, he would always 'accidentally' take her too far beyond the agreed distance, with the result that she became very frightened and tearful and consequently had to be rescued by her 'strong, caring' husband.

Eventually, Jenny could see what was happening and informed James quite calmly that he would have to leave if he didn't play his part in her recovery. This resulted in James becoming quite depressed and desperate to save his relationship. In therapy, it transpired that James overvalued strength and abhorred weakness in himself. In order to maintain this rigid one-sided view of himself, he had to see himself as strong and his wife as weak. He projected, if you will, the idea and reality of his own weakness on to Jenny, which enabled him to play the strong husband. It was only when James accepted himself as an unrateable, fallible human being who had strengths and weaknesses, and acknowledged that he did not have to exclude the latter from either his functioning or his awareness, that he began to make progress. Once he had began to make progress with himself, he could not only tolerate strength in Jenny, but could also facilitate and benefit from her strengths.

Whenever I work with couples where one partner embodies a quality and the other embodies its opposite, I am alert to the possibility that one or both people are desperate to expel the quality that he or she claims not to have, and I know that projecting it on to the partner is a very commonly used defensive manoeuvre in the expulsion process. This desperate attempt to expel the unwanted quality is based on the rigid idea that the person concerned must not have this quality or anything resembling it and would be a thoroughly despicable person if he or she did have it.

The key to helping couples with this issue is to encourage them to accept themselves if it transpires that they do have the unwanted quality. Self-acceptance helps to promote both ownership of the unwanted quality and an understanding of the complex intrapersonal and interpersonal processes involved when one is intolerant of a part of oneself.

Tolerance and respect among psychotherapists
Many of you will recognise the influence of psychodynamic ideas and

terms in my description and analysis of disturbed couple relationships. What am I, a Rational Emotive Behaviour Therapist, doing drawing on the ideas of psychodynamic therapists? Surely I should be slagging them off? If I did so, I would be acting at variance with the main thrust of my argument in this lecture. To argue that REBT is good and that psychodynamic therapy is bad is to make the same all-or-nothing thinking error that I hold to be the root of many psychological ills. No, while I am happy to state publicly that I am an REBT therapist, and to argue in favour of its virtues, this does not mean that other approaches do not have their virtues. Thus, psychodynamic theory offers some surprising, but accurate, accounts of human dysfunction; for example, a recent study has shown that there is evidence that homophobic men are aroused by homosexual imagery in a way that is consistent with Freud's views. Person-centred therapy also has its virtues; its emphasis on the therapeutic relationship revolutionised the whole field and showed that it was not good for practitioners to hide behind the protective shield of professionalism.

I could go on, but I think I have made my point. One can practise on approach to therapy and still respect the contribution of other approaches. I would not like to see the future of our field being marked by a bland uniformity of theory and practice. Rather, I would like to see a diversity of ideas, along with tolerance and respect for the work of colleagues from different therapeutic traditions.

The importance of a 'both/and' approach to human life

This emphasis on recognising the strengths of counselling approaches other than one's own is an example of a both/and approach to life. This is in direct contrast to an either/or approach. Let me give a few examples of both approaches, starting with one from our field.

There are those who emphasise the differences among approaches to counselling and psychotherapy. Such people know – or think they know – that their approach is the best approach, and they tend to denigrate what others have to offer. Other people in the field focus on similarity among approaches, and their *cri de coeur* is that research evidence indicates that different approaches can yield the same outcome. Both of these are examples of the either/or approach.

By contrast, those who take a both/and approach have their therapeutic preferences, but recognise the value of other approaches. They see both the differences and the similarities among the available approaches and argue that the research evidence shows that there are therapies of choice for various client problems, while for other problems different therapies will achieve comparable results.

Let me now change tack and consider one of the most important tasks that we have as humans. I refer to the ability of humans to be both separate from others and to be connected with others. Separateness is important for sustaining our unique identity, while connectedness is important for sustaining growth-enhancing intimacy with others. While both/and approach to separateness and connectedness can help people on the path to self-actualisation, an either/or approach to these conditions can lead to a variety of client problems.

Those who emphasise separateness to the exclusion of connectedness do not seek counselling as often as those who emphasise connectedness to the exclusion of separateness. However, they are often complained about by clients with whom they are in a relationship. The clients see them as closed off and unable to respond emotionally when this is appropriate. Such people tend to see all relationships in functional, highly stereotyped terms and do not view other people as a source of growth and development. The professional literature refers to those at the extreme of the separateness domain as schizoid. Such people erect rigid boundaries between themselves and others and often see relationships as a threat to their autonomy and identity. Their basic fear concerning relationships is engulfment.

Those who emphasise connectedness at the expense of separateness are overly focused on relationships as a source of identity. Some may even view relationship roles as synonymous with their identity (e.g. husband/wife; mother/father; son/daughter). Such people find it very difficult to tolerate being on their own and are often quite needy once they become related. Indeed, they tend to seek emotional sustenance from those with whom they are functionally related (e.g. their boss, teacher, doctor). Such people have highly permeable boundaries between themselves and others and often see the absence of relationships as a threat to their identity. Their basic fear concerning relationships is abandonment and isolation.

People who have a both/and approach to separateness and connectedness are comfortable both in relationships and on their own. They can pursue non-relationship activities and can easily return to their relationships when it is appropriate to do so. They can express themselves both emotionally and functionally according to the nature of the relationship that they are involved in. They tend to be intimate in intimate relationships and functional in functional relationships.

People with a both/and approach to separateness and connectedness tend to have a flexible approach to boundaries. When necessary they can erect firm boundaries between themselves and others, while at other times their interpersonal boundaries can be healthily permeable as they let others into their personal space as an expression of their commitment to these significant others.

Another example of a both/and approach to life is illustrated by people who can admit to themselves and to others that they can both succeed and fail at important tasks. Such people tend to learn from their failures and take healthy risks as they strive for what is important to them. They regard themselves not as either successes or failures but as unique, unrateable, fallible human beings who incorporate both their successes and their failures into their construct system. On the other hand, people with an either/or approach to this issue tend to see failure as something to be avoided at all costs and as constituting their identity if they encounter it. Such people are fearful about taking sensible risks and are frequently indecisive as they wait fruitlessly for a course of action to appear which guarantees them success. As many student counsellors will testify, even the most brilliant of individuals are not immune from this either/or approach to success and failure. Indeed, they are sometimes the very people who hold to this black and white ideology most rigidly.

One of my clients has spent most of her life in either/or territory. When she is in work mode, she rarely takes lunch or tea breaks and is often up half the night finishing some project or other. However, when she is at play nothing must interfere with her leisure. She has spent many years oscillating from stringent dieting to enormous bingeing and everything is either wonderful or terrible. Those of you who have worked with clients struggling with bulimia nervosa will not be surprised to learn that she has suffered from this disorder. This client, who is currently struggling to experience life from a both/and perspective, recently came up with a vivid phrase which has remained with me ever since. She calls her problem "bulimia lifeosa" and sees this as the antithesis to the balanced and flexible approach to life that she is striving to adopt. I think that this phrase says it all, don't you?

Some shocking implications

Let me now discuss some shocking implications of the ideas that I have presented so far. The first concerns what has been called political correctness, a term that I will use here to include its offshoots, 'emotional correctness' and 'therapeutic correctness'.

As a counsellor trainer, I have seen the effects of internalised political correctness as trainees exercise great caution in what they say for fear of offending other trainees or their trainers. If trainees cannot take risks on counselling courses and express their real feelings, even if these feelings may be examples of racism, sexism or any other -ism, where *can* they express themselves? My fear is that, under the tyranny of political correctness, trainees will not only keep their true feelings from their fellow trainees and from their trainers, but also will learn to hide these feelings from themselves. Thus, for me, good counsellor trainers establish a climate where politically incorrect views can be tolerated and explored and where the trainees expressing them can be accepted before their views are challenged. Otherwise, we will be training a generation of counsellors who will be constantly monitoring what they say and feel to see if it is acceptable to the prevailing zeitgeist.

This is not to say that I want to unleash on to the world counsellors who hold racist and sexist views. It is just that I think that, unless these views can be uttered, they cannot be usefully explored and integrated into the totality of the person. Note that I said 'integrated' and not 'expunged'. That is the crucial point.

The second shocking implication of my views concerns an experience that a minority of women who have been sexually abused have had, but rarely talk about. Such women, to their horror, have found elements of the total experience enjoyable and some may have even have experienced an orgasm during the abuse. This is rare, but it does happen. By acknowledging the existence of this phenomenon, I am in no way minimising the aversiveness of the abuse, blaming the victim or reducing the culpability of the person responsible for the abuse.

It is in the unpredictable nature of human responsiveness that we can have an experience that we certainly don't want (like having an orgasm in the course of an abusive attack) and we may not have an experience that we actively do want (like having an orgasm with our partner during lovemaking). Helping women who have had an orgasm in the course of an abusive attack to understand this perverse fact of human life, and to acknowkedge that human sexual response, like other areas of human endeavour, is unpredictable, fluid and paradoxical, can be enormously therapeutic for them and can encourage them to view the situation in a much broader context than they have often done hitherto. Previously, they may have seen their orgasmic response as casting doubt on their motives, behaviour and even their identity (e.g. 'Maybe I wanted it to happen', 'Maybe I encouraged him in some way' or even 'What a sick person I am to feel this at that time'). And previously they have had a common-sense, but incorrect, either/or view of sexual response; e.g., 'If you love someone you have an orgasm with him. You just don't have an orgasm during sexual abuse.' Here is a clear example where the either/or approach leads to disturbance and the both/and approach leads to a therapeutic resolution.

You may be wondering why I decided to entitle this talk 'Looking for the Good in Hitler and Acknowledging the Bad in Mother Teresa'. Well, your wait is over, for the time has come for me to tackle this delicate subject. So far in this talk I have argued that a both/and way of approaching human experience yields better results than an either/or approach. Following from this, I will now argue that Hitler was not all bad, nor Mother Teresa all good. We may need to see them as all bad and all good respectively, but this says more about us than it does about them.

Let me briefly review some of Hitler's better qualities. He was a very good organiser and a very good public speaker. He showed great bravery in the First World War, capturing several enemy soldiers single-handedly. He was capable of love and was kind to animals. Please do not think that by saying these things I am a neo-Nazi or an apologist for Hitler. He did, of course, do immense harm to Jews, of whom I am one, to gypsies and to homosexuals. I do not absolve him from the responsibility for any of this, but the fact of the matter is that he was not *all* bad. If he was, he would not have been human.

You may have heard that Mother Teresa is on the fast-track to being made a saint by Rome. Her name is synonymous with goodness, and there is no doubt that her devoted efforts have brought succour to countless people over the years. But was she all good? Far from it. Her hospitals were poorly stocked with medical supplies and were often kept in a bare and freezing state – this despite the fact that her mission received very generous financial support from many quarters.

Also, despite publicly stating that she would not accept money from the rich, she received donations amounting to $1.25 million from Charles Keating, who was sent to prison for ten years for fraud. Mother Teresa sent an unsolicited letter to the trial judge to ask for clemency. When the deputy district attorney in Los Angeles County wrote to Mother Teresa explaining the facts of the case and requesting that she return the money donated to her by Keating, money that he stole from ordinary, working people, Mother Teresa did not respond.

In addition, perhaps because of her respected position, Mother Teresa's accounts were never audited, and thus, large sums of money sent by her to 'her headquarters in Rome' have never been explained. I could go on, and those of you who are interested in learning more should read a book entitled *The Missionary Position: Mother Teresa in Theory and Practice* by Christopher Hitchens (1995). Unfortunately, in his zeal to expose the 'sins' of Mother Teresa, Hitchens takes an either/or approach and fails to consider and evaluate her good works. My purpose in mentioning this lesser-known side of Mother Teresa is not to discredit her, but to place her in full context, to acknowledge the bad in her as well as the good.

My point is that Hitler was not evil and Mother Teresa was not a saint. Hitler had his good side and Mother Teresa her bad. In taking this stance I do not for one minute wish to excuse Hitler for his crimes against humanity, nor do I wish to detract from Mother Teresa's good works. Rather, I wish to make the point that both were human and have features that we all share.

Conclusion

In conclusion, let me say that one of our tasks as human beings is to accept that we are capable of experiencing the entire range of human reactions and responses. We are all capable of the greatest of good and the vilest of evil. To use jargon for a moment, we all have a Hitler inside us as well as a Mother Teresa. If we fully accept ourselves as such, we can learn to maximise the good in ourselves and to minimise the bad. However, if we try to expel our bad unwanted side, and in particular if we attempt to do so in a desperate manner, we create problems both for ourselves and for those with whom we come into contact. If we accept ourselves as fallible human beings capable of experiencing the entire range of human functioning, and if we accept others as similar to ourselves in this respect, such acceptance will promote understanding and even compassion.

It is this understanding and compassion that is in desperate short supply as we approach the millenium. Is it naive and idealistic of me to hope that, if we can accept ourselves and others as fallible human beings, this will help us to live more peaceably with ourselves and with others? For our future, I trust it is not.

Reference

Hitchens, C. (1995). *The missionary position: Mother Teresa in theory and practice.* London: Verso.

index

ABC theory 49
audiotapes in counselling 90
awfulising 116, 139
    anti- 116
Bannister, D. 61, 73
being a client 70
Bentine, M. 42
Biggs, D. 37
Birmingham Marriage Guidance 89
blame 130
Bond, F.W. 51, 144, 145, 150
'both/and' approach to human life 160
Bordin, E.S. 54, 56, 116, 123
Bourneville College 59
British Association for Counselling 21
    Code of Ethics and Practice 3
British Psychological Society 114, 123,
    137
    Code of Conduct, 114
bulimia lifeosa 162
Carkhuff, R. 19
challenging 14
change
    and half-hearted action 128
    personal 129
Christ 145, 146
Church,V.A. 41
client
    obstacles to change 15, 16
    past attempts at solving
    problems 15
    stage of change 15
    tasks 63
        educating in their 62
    training 66
    unique set of circumstances 13
Clinical Theology Association 59
connectedness 161
Conservative Party 144
contracts 3
control 82
counselling profile 23

Counselling Psychology
    1st International Conference 137
counsellor
    role 64, 113
        explaining the 64
    tasks 65, 114, 117
        in couple counselling 92
couple
    conflict 157
    counselling 92–98
    disturbance 90
        ABC's of 95
        distinction between 93
    dissatisfaction 90
        ABC's of 95
        distinction between 93
Coxhead, P. 21, 24
discomfort disturbance 52
Demandingness 116
De Michele, J.T. 17, 24
Depreciating 116
Di Clemente, C.C. 15, 24
dogmatism 157
Dryden, W. 17, 21, 23, 24, 28, 34, 48,
    51, 56, 57, 62, 73, 77, 96, 98, 127,
    136, 145
eclectic and integrative approach 22
ego disturbance 52
Ellis, A. 14, 41, 42, 43, 47, 48, 54, 55,
    56, 71, 73, 96, 98, 105, 108, 110
emotional destiny 130
emotions
    negative 50
empathy 37
empowering 18, 49
ending 20
European Association for Counselling 59
evaluation 31
feeling reactions to clients 17
Feltham, C. 1
focus of counselling 10
follow-up sessions 20

Freud, S. 146, 160
frustration tolerance
 high 117
 low 116, 139
Garfield, S.L. 63, 74
Garvin, C.D. 70, 74
genuineness 37
Gloria 41, 47
goal directedness 8
Harper, R. 41, 43, 71, 73
Hartop, B. 1
Hauck, P. 51, 57, 102, 110, 130
heterosexual male sexuality 153
high frustration tolerance 117
Hill, C.E. 17, 24
Hitchens, C. 164, 165
Hitler, A. 163, 164, 165
Holocaust 6, 142, 144
homosexuality 153
Hunt, P.A. 91, 98
Institute for Rational-Emotive Therapy 41
implicit tasks 62
informed consent 63
intellectual insight 53
irrational beliefs 54
influence
 compromises in the process of
 REBT and 119
 dangers of using 121
Jourard , S. 38, 43
Keating, C 164
Kunzel, R. 24
Kushlik, A. 45
Lake, F. 59
Lazarus, A. 6, 21, 23, 102, 110
Life History Inventory 21
lobbying 33
low frustration tolerance 116, 139
Magnusson, M. 146, 150
managed care 32
marketing 33
Maultsby, M. C. Jr 41, 61, 74
Mearns, D. 113, 123
meta-emotional problems 53
Miller, D.J. 3, 24

Moore, J. 151
Mother Teresa 163, 164, 165
National Marriage Guidance Council
 34, 89
Neenan, M. 105, 110
Nelson-Jones, R.19, 21, 24, 37, 38, 61,
 74
non-absolute preferences 116
Norcross, J.C. 17, 24
Obsessive Action 75
obsessive-compulsive disorder 75, 77–85
 REBT's contribution to 84
 risk appraisal 77
obsessive thoughts 153
cbstacles to change 15
 clients' 15, 16
Oedipus 146-149
 complex 146
Olins, R. 89
Open Door 27–34
parents 154
 being different from 154
Patterson, C. 109, 110
Pepping, G. 24
Perls 41, 47
person-centred therapy 160
political correctness 162
Prochasks, J.O. 15, 24
Proctor, B. 37
professional knowledge 21
protestant ethic 54
psychodynamic therapy 40, 42, 160
psycho-educational approach 55, 63-74
 advantages 72
 criticisms 72
psychological disturbance 48, 116
psychological education 61
psychological health 116
questionnaires 21
rape 139
Rational Emotive Behaviour Therapy
 41, 47-57,
 and couple counselling 92-98
rational beliefs 53, 54
referral 6

reflection 4
Regan, A.M. 17, 24
relapse 19
Relate 34, 89-98
relationship actualisation 97
research findings 21
responsibility 77, 130
review 7
Rogers, C.R. 28, 34, 37, 38, 39, 41, 42,
    44, 47, 55, 57, 90, 113, 114, 123
Schofield, W. 113, 123
Seabury, B.A 70, 74
self 51
self-acceptance 51, 117
self-actualisation 113
self-control 155, 156
    fear of losing 155
self-esteem 51, 102
    low 101
    raising 103
self-fulfilling prophecy 130
self-help books 125-136
    and the search for magic 129
    limitations of 134
    qualities of good 135
    reading for change 128
self-reflection 21
self-supervision 23
separateness 161
shoulds 141–150
Shulte, D. 22, 24
splitting 157
Strean, H.S. 4, 24
structuring 9
supervision 23
tasks
    change-enhancing 12
    client's 63
    client and therapist 114, 117
    counsellor's 65, 114, 117
    educating clients in their 62
    implicit 62
teaching the REBT framework 114
tender-minded counselling qualities 28
Thelen, M.H. 3, 24
therapeutic alliance 54

therapeutic bond 6
therapeutic change 53
    positive 53
    negative 53
things left unsaid 17
thinking the unthinkable 144
Thorne, B. J. 113, 123, 151
Tjeltveit, A.C. 114, 123
tolerance and respect among psycho-
    therapists 159
tough-minded counselling practices 31
training clients 66
Truax, C.B. 114, 124
Uffculme Clinic 39, 40
unconditional positive regard 37
unconditional positive self-esteem 108
unconditional self-acceptance 52, 106
    teaching 108
United Kingdom Council for Psycho-
    therapy 33, 34
Universities Psychotherapy Association
    111
University of Aston in Birmingham 37,
    61
University of Durham 1
University of East Anglia 151
University of London School for
    Oriental and African Studies 111
value conversion 114
Veale, D. Dr. 75
Walker, A. 49
working through 30
Yankura, J. 48, 57

Person-Centred Approach
& Client-Centred Therapy
Essential Reader

Person-Centred Therapy
A Revolutionary Paradigm

by Jerold Bozarth

Professor Jerold Bozarth worked with Carl Rogers from 1974 to 1987. In this book he presents a collection of revised papers and new writings on Person-Centred therapy representing over 40 years' work as an innovator and theoretician. This book is essential reading for all with an interest in Client-Centred Therapy and the Person-Centred Approach.

• • •

SACRED SCIENCE
Person-centred Inquiry into the Spiritual and the Subtle

by John Heron

John Heron writes: *'This book is about my own lived inquiry in the spiritual and subtle field, about a radical revision of transpersonal theory, and about a pioneer form of sacred science in which human beings co-operate together to inquire in a rigorous manner into their own spiritual and subtle experience, without prior allegiance to any existing school.'*

• • •

IMPLAUSIBLE PROFESSIONS
Arguments for Pluralism and Autonomy in Psychotherapy and Counselling

edited by Richard House and Nick Totton

'At last a book on counselling and psychotherapy that demands to be read. A book that wasn't commissioned by Sage, isn't written by big name trainers for captive students, but one that is compelling, uncomfortable, uneven, likely to be unpopular in some quarters, and is unequivocally passionate committed and honest. . .What you get here is a lot of what Virginia Satir once called 'levelling' - telling the honest truth. . .Together they [the authors] demonstrate the persistence in many humanistic practitioners of a deep tenacity and groundedness that resist the creeping 'McDonaldisation' of the treatment of contemporary woe that the professionalisation process has ushered in.'
David Kalisch *Self & Society March 1998*